M000045978

WORDS

They
Become
You

LISA SINGH

WORDS
Copyright © 2015 Inspirations by Lisa

All rights reserved. No portion of this book may be reproduced, stored in a retrieval system, or transmitted in any form or by any means—electronic, mechanical, photocopy, recording, scanning, or other—except for brief quotations in critical reviews or articles, without the prior written permission of the author.

© Cover Image: image copyright Ase, used under license from Shutterstock.com.

Scripture quotations marked "The Amplified Bible" (AMP) or "The Amplified New Testament" are taken from The Amplified Bible, Old Testament copyright © 1965, 1987 by the Zondervan Corporation and "The Amplified Classic Version" (AMPC) by The Lockman Foundation. Used by permission. All rights reserved.

Scripture quotations marked (NIV®) are taken from the HOLY BIBLE, NEW INTERNATIONAL VERSION ®. NIV®. Copyright © 1973, 1978, 1984 by International Bible Society. Used by permission. All rights reserved worldwide.

Scripture taken from the New King James Version marked (NKJV). Copyright © 1982 by Thomas Nelson, Inc. Used by permission. All rights reserved.

Scripture quotations from *THE MESSAGE*. Copyright © by Eugene H. Peterson 1993, 1994, 1995, 1996, 2000, 2001, 2002. Used by permission of NavPress Publishing Group.

Dedication

I would like to dedicate this book first to the Holy Spirit, who is the greatest inspiration in my life. His wisdom, guidance and patience with me are overwhelming, and this book definitely could not have manifested without His help. Secondly, I would like to dedicate this book to my family and my HGM leadership for allowing me the time I needed to write, by sharing in the responsibilities; thereby allowing me the opportunity to reach more souls. May the grace and peace of our Lord Jesus Christ be overly abundant in your lives!

Table of Contents

Introduction

Introduction

Words, words, words, we use them all the time, but have you ever wondered where your words go? Do they just disappear into thin air or just fade away? Well, about two years ago, I started to notice certain things were happening in my life that was resulting in negative effects. Being a Pastor, my foundation is established on a solid prayer life, at least I thought so, but I could not figure out why everything seemed to be going so wrong. Of course, the only logical explanation was to blame it on the devil because, after all, he is the source of confusion. Now, I know I am not the only one that does that, right now you might be smiling because you know you have taken that route as well. No condemnation, it happens to all of us. I decided to seek the Lord for the answer to why everything was going so wrong in my life, and the Lord's response was so simple yet very shocking. He said, "Lisa, your words!" So I stood there waiting for more but nothing else came. For days, those three words haunted me, and I decided to venture out on a mission to find out all I can about words. By now you should be able to figure out that the topic of "words": not only intrigued me but changed my life. I want to take the time to present to you and even suggest that not everything happening in your life is because of the devil or a demon while the devil does look for opportunities to wreak havoc in your life we must first give him that chance to do so. I have come to realize that many of the issues of life we face can easily be traced back to our words. Dr. Louann Brizendine in her book, *The Female Brain* states, *"On average girls speak two to three times more words per day than boys."* What a disparity? I guess that would explain the fall in the Garden, Eve talked twice as much as Adam; thereby bringing down the whole world with one conversation. Do you get the gist? Words are very powerful; words create and build up or pull down and destroy. In other words; words can mean life or death. According to Ask.com, a study from a University in Arizona found that most people speak about 16,000 words a day. Just think about it for a moment, if you are a woman, there is a probability you send out about two to three times more words a day than men and on a general basis you speak roughly 16,000 words in a day, regardless of your gender. In all those words you speak, ask yourself, "What am I creating, since words do not disappear?" It's a sobering question, I know. But it is time for us to take this journey together and find freedom from the many prisons we have created for ourselves by our words.

Our words and our thoughts are tied to each other because the Bible states, "*A good man out of the good treasure of his heart brings forth good; and an evil man out of the evil treasure of his heart brings forth evil. For out of the abundance of the heart his mouth speaks*" (Luke 6:45 NKJV). Then it states again, "*So then faith comes by hearing, and hearing by the word of God*" (Romans 10:17 NKJV). So, from these two Scriptures, it will be safe to establish that words create thoughts and thoughts give way to words; in essence without first hearing words, you really can't have thought. How powerful is that? For many years, or should I say all my life, I have heard that you must change your thinking before you can change your life, and that is true but, in my studies on this topic of words I have found that the absolute about changing your mind has everything to do with the words you are hearing. It all comes back to words! During this book, I will repeat this principle because I want change to come to your lives. Unfortunately, we have not come to understand the power we hold as children of God and my hope is to help you become all you can be by using your words wisely. The good news is you can start today to reshape and reconstruct your life, and the world around you, by just making a simple choice to change the way you speak. Are you ready? Then turn the page!

Chapter 1

What are Words?

In the beginning [before all time] was the Word (Christ), and the Word was with God, and the Word was God Himself (John 1:1 AMP).

"Words are a spiritual force. They are containers shaped by our thoughts, intentions, and meaning-tools that chisel our lives and the lives of those around us into masterpieces"—Dr. Cindy Trimm

From the above Scripture, the Greek word for "word" is *logos*, and it means "a word, speech, divine utterance, analogy and is preeminently used of Christ, expressing the thoughts of the Father through the Spirit."

I know you might be wondering why all this "Greek," but therein lies the principle of life and creativity. Logos denotes "the expression of thought," and it was by the expression of God's thoughts that we see the world as we know it. God created everything good, and He did it all by the "Logos"—Christ.

By faith, we understand that the worlds [during the successive ages] were framed (fashioned, put in order, and equipped for their intended purpose) by the word of God, so that what we see was not made out of things that are visible (Hebrews 11:3 AMP).

In the very first Book of the Bible, Genesis, Chapter 1, we see the whole creative process of the heaven and earth. And what is most interesting in the creative process is the unity of the God-head. This first chapter tells us the Spirit of God was hovering, or brooding, over the waters; God came on the scene and spoke what was in His mind and the Word—Jesus, displayed the mind of God. Everything God created in Chapter One, except for man, God spoke it into being. Not only that, but the Bible tells us that when God spoke it, then he saw it, and approved it as good. What you have to understand here is that God's ways are very different from the world's ways. The world lives by the principle of "you have to see it to believe it," but God's principle is to "believe it then you will see it."

And God saw everything that He had made, and behold, it was very good (suitable, pleasant) and He approved it completely. And there was evening, and there was morning, a sixth day (Genesis 1:31 AMP).

I would like to bring to your attention, in this first chapter of Genesis, where God stepped into chaos, darkness, confusion, formlessness, no order and no governance. Here is how the Message Bible describes it, *"First this: God created the Heavens and Earth—all you see, all you don't see. Earth was a soup of nothingness, a bottomless emptiness, an inky blackness. God's Spirit brooded like a bird above the watery abyss"* (Genesis 1:1 MSG). What I'm trying to show you is that God began with nothing but chaos—He did not step into something a bit, run down and realize that He had to repair it. His starting point was the worst of the worst state of affairs. He had to bring something out of nothing; we also have issues present in our lives that are chaotic, confusing and unbalanced, but we already have something to work with, and the same concept that God used is the same concept available to us. Today, your broken relationship or marriage might be that bottomless, emptiness; or maybe a failing business, perhaps a disease in your body or major financial stresses, a rebellious child or an addict in your home...maybe domestic violence or the loss of your job. Our chaos and confusion can appear in many different forms, but the principle for dealing with it all remains the same. It would then stand to reason that if we are created in the image and likeness of God, with that same ability to believe and speak the logos, with the help of the Holy Spirit, the ability to bring about results from doing so resides in us as well. My friends, it's the same God-head that is existent today—the Father, Son and Holy Spirit...and mind you, they still work together for God's will to be fulfilled in the lives of those who will accept the way of Jesus. With this amazing truth, the question remains, "Why so many believers are living defeated?" Why so much sickness, disease, depression, failure, fear, anxiety, worry, sleepless nights, rebelliousness and divorce? Why can't we grasp freedom and victory even though we go to church, pray, worship and praise? The answer, my friends, can be traced back to the little part of the body called the tongue.

What did Jesus say about words?
Jesus said,
"My Words are spirit and life."

Let us look at the words of Jesus...He said, *"It is the Spirit who gives life; the flesh profits nothing. The words that I speak to you are spirit, and they are life"* (John 6:63 NKJV). From this Scripture, we can clearly establish that there are "life" words and there are "death" words, and Jesus emphatically establishes that His words are "spirit" and "life." But whether the words are "life" words or "death" words, both are "Spirit" words. We don't see words when we speak them, but yet they can create or destroy in the same way we don't see angels or demons, unless they manifest through a tangible body—it's the same way words work. They exist in the spirit form, until the time of manifestation—be it life or death. In her book, *Commanding your Morning*, Dr. Cindy Trimm describes words this way, *"Words released into the atmosphere do not disappear and dissipate. They have no geographical limitations. Words have power, presence, and prophetic implications. They create a magnetic force that pulls the manifestation of what you speak-good or bad, blessing or cursing-from other realms, regions, and dimensions. They are suspended and incubated in the realm of the spirit awaiting the correct time and optimum condition for manifestation."* It would stand to reason, that if we are not aligning ourselves with Jesus' words, we are not aligning ourselves with "life." And this would explain why our prayer lives are weak, our walk is defeated, our bodies are sick, our tempers flare, unforgiveness and bitterness are rampant in our lives, and we lack financially. I believe it has everything to do with the words we are releasing around us on a daily basis, and because we have not fully understood that our words are Spirit waiting to manifest, we continue to release them carelessly. While the enemy is the source of confusion and he comes to steal from us, I want you to understand that he cannot do anything unless you give him what he needs to do it. Once we put words out into the atmosphere, he then has something to work with because through our speech he hears what is in our hearts and then he plots and plans to bring attacks. Be assured, the devil cannot read your mind, only God knows your heart, thoughts, and intentions. The enemy pays close attention to what is coming out of your mouth because he is always looking for ammunition to come against you. In the same way, "death" words empower the enemy, so "life" words empower the angels of God. The writer of Hebrews presents a question, *"Are not all angels ministering spirits sent to serve those who will inherit salvation"* (Hebrews 1:14 NIV)? And then King David said, *"Bless the LORD, you His angels, Who excel in strength, who do His word, Heeding the voice of His word"* (Psalm 103:20 NKJV). Clearly, from these two Scriptures, we can see we have help from the Kingdom of God, and the angels also excel in strength when we speak God's words. I am very hopeful by the end of this book that you will be transformed in your speech and equipped in your knowledge of words. I pray the life Jesus talks about and the life He came to give you would fully manifest itself in this natural realm.

Jesus said,
"Words come back to haunt you."

I have personally tested and tried this by default, and I will share with you all how, later on in the book, but for now I want you to know that your words will eventually come back to haunt you. Jesus had some very weighty words about words when he addressed the religious leaders of His day. He said, *"If you grow a healthy tree, you'll pick healthy fruit. If you grow a diseased tree, you'll pick worm-eaten fruit. The fruit tells you about the tree. You have minds like a snake pit! How do you suppose what you say is worth anything when you are so foul-minded? It's your heart, not the dictionary, that gives meaning to your words. A good person produces good deeds and words season after season. An evil person is a blight on the orchard. Let me tell you something: Every one of these careless words is going to come back to haunt you. There will be a time of Reckoning. Words are powerful; take them seriously. Words can be your salvation. Words can also be your damnation"* (Matthew 12:33-37 MSG).

We must look carefully at the description Jesus uses as He likens us to trees and He shows us how we can identify a good tree or a bad tree—it all has to do with the fruit it produces. Jesus also draws the connection between the heart and our words. What Jesus said is so powerful that I have to state it again for your attention: He said, *"It's your heart, not the dictionary, that gives meaning to your words. A good person produces good deeds and words season after season"* (Matthew 12:35 MSG). The words you are speaking have everything to do with what is inside of you—your belief system. It is from this system that things will grow or die. If the Word of God is in our heart, then we cannot help but produce good fruit; but if the works of the flesh are in our hearts...like bitterness, anger, jealousy, covetousness, etc., then there is no way we can produce good fruit. Unfortunately, in today's world and culture, we have become so preoccupied with the outside that we fix everything to be attractive to the natural eye, while we terribly neglect the heart condition. It's like sticking a plastic fruit to a real tree so it can appear as if it is real, but we all know in real life that the fake fruit will eventually fall off, and it will be of no value to anyone. I usually like to say if you want to know what someone thinks just listen long enough, and you will be able to identify the thoughts and intents of the person. I also believe the reason we make so many mistakes and align our-selves sometimes with the wrong crowd is because we hardly ever take any time to listen to the heart of the person. Jesus explained that words get meaning from what's going on in the heart—not a dictionary. Many of us get duped in life and hurt in life because we are drawn in by sweet and eloquent words spoken by people that appear to be genuine, but in reality they are fake. Jesus warns us, from the above Scripture, to pay attention to the fruit the tree is producing because that is the key to identifying what is genuine and what is not. He also warns us to take our words seriously be-cause they will one day come back to haunt us. You have to recognize that words never really disappear into thin air; but rather are waiting and will eventually attach to what it was sent to produce and manifest itself—be it in life or death or as Jesus states, *"Salvation or damnation"* (Matthew 12:37).

Jesus said, *"Do not worry."*

I know "Do not worry" sounds like it's off topic, since we're talking about words...but what does worry have to do with our words? I'm glad you asked, because I know this will open your eyes to one of the main rea-sons we are so anxious and worried all the time. In Je-sus' Sermon on the Mount, one of the topics He sheds light on is the "worrying" aspect. It's an issue that is plaguing almost every human being in one form or an-other. We worry about our health, finances, education, our children, the future, relationships, careers, and meeting our daily needs—all of these things trigger fear and anxiety because of all the unknowns. The enemy loves to get us worried, because once we are busy worrying, he knows we won't be praying, praising or worshipping. I have heard the Sermon on the Mount practically my whole life, but I never really paid much attention to the details of the words in this particular teaching. Jesus was teaching about life and the needs that arise on a daily basis like food and clothes. We cannot survive without food, at least not for a long period, and it would prove to be inappropriate to go about in public without clothes. In essence, Jesus knew that these essentials are a big deal for every human, and he takes the time to address it to show us how much our Father loves us. He makes a comparison to the birds of the air and the flower of the fields, to us—his children. He explains that the birds do not have a barn anywhere to store up food, and they have no jobs, they don't get paid, so they can't meet their needs; and yet our Heavenly Father feeds, and sustains them. Then, He shows how the flowers of the fields are so beautiful and radiant in vibrant colors, and they also do not have jobs to purchase clothes, reiterating that our Heavenly Father clothes them, even though their life span can sometimes be only a day or two (see Matthew 6:25–34). After Jesus draws this comparison of the birds and flowers to us, He says something most remarkable—let us examine what He said, "Therefore do not worry, **saying**, "'What shall we eat?' or 'What shall we drink?' or 'What shall we wear?'" (Matthew 6:31 NKJV) Jesus linked our worry to what we say, did you get that? We give weight and shape and body to our worries when we voice those worries or put words to those worries. I have heard an old saying, "You can't stop a bird from flying over your head, but you can stop the bird from building a nest in your hair." This statement holds so much weight because the truth is we can't stop thoughts from entering our mind, but we can, most assuredly, refuse to let those thoughts stay. Once we voice our thoughts we give them permission to manifest. Jesus was showing us the moment we say things like, "What am I going to do with all this debt I'm in?" "What will happen if I lose my job or my house?" or "What will I do if God does not meet my needs for this month", we are putting things in motion to block His hand of provision, healing and protection in our lives. Worry will always be there; it will always try to break down the door of your mind and try to get into your heart. Worry will try to kill the very joy of your present. But, the Apostle Paul gives us a wonderful strategy to deal with worry, he said, *"Don't fret or worry. Instead of worrying, pray. Let petitions and praises shape your worries into prayers, letting God know your concerns"* (Philippians 4:6 MSG). Paul uses the same pattern of speaking words to counteract worry; instead of voicing the worry, he encourages us to shape the thoughts of worry in our minds into prayers and praises and then speak those out unto God. He goes on to tell us that God's peace will come in the midst of the praise and settle our hearts down. Look at what he said, *"Before you know it, a sense of God's wholeness, everything coming together for good, will come and settle you down. It's wonderful what happens when Christ displaces worry at the center of your life"* (Philippians 4:7 MSG). You see my friends, you have an answer to the worry that seeks to paralyze you, when you find thoughts come to mind like, "How am I going to pay that bill?", you follow the pattern that Paul presents and shape your thought into a prayer by saying,

Father, I come to You because Your Word says I can come into Your throne room and ask for help. I have this bill due, and I do not have the monies to pay it, but I also know that Your Word assures me that You will provide all my needs according to Your riches in glory. I will not worry today, but I am thanking You in advance for the door You will open to allow this bill to be paid, in Jesus name, Amen. Now as you go on your way during the day, this worrying thought will try again to enter your mind and at those moments you practice to stay in a place of thanksgiving, continuing to thank God for the need to be met. Once you don't voice the worry, but replace it with prayer and praise, that need is going to be met because God now has room to work a miracle. Give him a chance to work in your life by simply pushing worry aside with words of prayer and praise!

Jesus said,
"Faith words will move mountains."

He said to them, "*Because of the littleness of your faith [that is, your lack of firmly relying trust]. For truly I say to you, if you have faith [that is living] like a grain of mustard seed, you can say to this mountain, Move from here to yonder place, and it will move; and nothing will be impossible to you*" (Matthew 17:20 AMP).

You will have to agree with me that moving a mountain is an impossible task; can you imagine standing at the bottom of Mount Everest and trying to move it to get to your destination? Jesus explains to His disciples that moving a mountain is possible, and He says nothing about excavating it with equipment and machines, but rather gives them a simple, and in layman terms, silly solution of speaking to it. While he used a material substance of a mountain to make his point, I think it was the aspect of the impossibility that Jesus was trying to reference. Today, it is not literal mountains that stand in our way, but life issues that are equivalent to the weight and size of mountains that keep us down...like debilitating pain in our bodies, an alcoholic spouse, a violent home, lack of finances for a proper education and the list can go on. Jesus, in knowing the pressures of everyday life, wanted us to know that faith and trust in Him will make the mountains of life move, but please pay attention to the truth contained within the statement—it is not just faith in Him, but when your faith is activated by speaking, then it will move mountains. Kenneth E. Hagin, in his book, *Words*, stated, "Faith is always expressed in WORDS. Faith must be released in WORDS through your mouth." I have to say that many times we try to reason in the natural by being logical and faith cannot operate when we reason in the natural. Most times, when faced with a life issue like a bad report from the doctor, immediately we tend to reason it in the natural and at that moment we nullify our confidence and trust in God. Because of the fallen state of our world, the emotions of fear, worry and anxiety seem to come naturally. I am not downplaying pain, hurt or diseases because they are real, and a bad report can trigger any and all of the negative emotions. Here is where the faith factor comes in...rather than giving into the emotions, by speaking it out, we go to the words of God and speak those out in faith, and this is the way we counteract the negatives that life tries to throw at us. We must learn how to remain in faith, and we do so by speaking God's words!

Jesus also went on to say, *"The thief does not come except to steal, and to kill, and to destroy. I have come that they may have life and that they may have it more abundantly"* (John 10:10 NKJV). Everything about Jesus' mission was restoration and life and establishing the kingdom of God. He preached good news—life words and these words set captives free, opened blind eyes and ears, both literally and spiritually. He never gave diseases to anyone, He multiplied where there was lack, and he raised the dead. Jesus lived the abundant life, and He came to teach us to have this abundant life as well. Notice the Scripture establishes that we, too, may have the same life; this is God's will for us. Jesus tells us that the enemy comes to steal, kill and destroy and the enemy does it in the same way—by "death" words. Yes, we see murders, sex trafficking, famine, poverty and wars around the world on a global scale. And it can be traced back to the work of the devil, but every day his mission is also to destroy the individual life by wreaking havoc in our marriages, our homes, our bodies, our businesses, our friendships and partnerships, our children and loved ones. He tries to kill our dreams, hopes and visions and he does it through the words we are speaking because of his infiltration of the human language. May this point ever be kept before you as you move on in life from today, Jesus' words are life, and they create life; the enemy words are death, and they bring death, whichever words you choose to speak you will determine if you bring life or death!

Prayer of Creative Words

Father, today I am determined to live by your principles, and I know I can do it because I have help from the Holy Spirit.

Father, I desire to transform my life, and I know it can be transformed by the words I speak.

Father, today I understand that Jesus is the Logos and by Him everything was created. Therefore, I will not speak idle words but I will speak creative words.

Father, I understand I am made in the image and likeness of you, and if you created the heaven and the earth out of chaos, then every chaotic situation in my life can change as well by my speaking.

Father, you have opened up my mind and eyes to see that my words carry power, and I refuse to waste the power of the spoken word on things that are of no value and that are temporary.

Father, I commit my mouth to you, and I ask that the words of my lips will be acceptable in your sight. Help me to remember always that words are spirit, and once they go out, they wait to produce and with this remembrance enable me to put life words in the atmosphere.

Father, today I am determined to be like the tree that brings forth good deeds and fruit in every season. I decree and declare that my fruit will be authentic.

Father, help me to be able to differentiate between good trees and bad trees that will come around my life today, let me no longer be blinded by just smooth words but allow me to see the heart.

Father, let my heart be made right as I focus on the words of Jesus, let the words that proceed out of my mouth originate from a heart that is saturated completely with the words of Christ.

Father, today I thank you that I can counteract worry by praying and praising instead of voicing my worries. I ask for your help Lord as I train my mind and heart to faith words rather than worry words.

Father, I am so blessed to have the spiritual reinforcements of the angelic host because I am a child of yours. Today I will empower the angels to work on my behalf by releasing your words, and I know that as I do this the forces of darkness will be rendered powerless.

Father, I thank you for helping me to understand that every word that Jesus spoke is spirit and life; today I will speak His words over all circumstances because it will bring dead things to life. Every dead situation will manifest to life in Jesus' name. Amen!

Chapter 2

Speaking is a Choice... Where Does Real Power Lie?

As we look around the world, it seems as if our minds are trained to believe that power lies in the hands of governments and nations, or the rich and famous, or maybe the educated, or even with a particular race of people. Some nations believe that the more weapons they own will eventually give them ultimate power, while some believe it would mean more land or more oil wells. Some individuals believe that if they have enough money they can buy their way to power and status and, of course, they believe that with this kind of power they can control people. Ultimately, the world's idea of power is to control the assets and thereby control the people. This definition of power sounds exactly like the devil's agenda, if you ask me. While there may be physical signs of power being existent from the list above, the Scriptures emphatically state that real power belongs to God and the words that come out of His mouth are most powerful. Jesus, in His moments of being tested in the wilderness, spoke these words to the devil, *"'Jesus answered, "It is written: 'Man shall not live on bread alone, but on every word that comes from the mouth of God'"* (Matthew 4:4 NIV). Clearly we have missed it somewhere, by believing that power lies in possessions, status and abundance...when truly, from Scriptures, we can see that *real* power lies in words and ultimate power is resident in God's words. Let us examine a little further on what the Scriptures say,

Death and life are in the power of the tongue, and they who indulge in it shall eat the fruit of it [for death or life] (Proverbs 18:21 AMP).

But, I particularly love The Message translation of this verse...look at it closely, it states, *"Words kill, words give life; they're either poison or fruit—you choose"* (Proverbs 18:21 MSG).

It is very clear from this Scripture, we have a choice in the matter of our words. King Solomon penned these words, and as far as we know, God blessed King Solomon with wisdom above all men that ever lived; in fact, God said to him, *"Behold, I have done as you asked. I have given you a wise, discerning mind, so that no one before you was your equal, nor shall any arise after you equal to you"* (1 Kings 3:12 AMP). With a blessing like that from God, I truly believe there will be much to learn from this wise king. I will come back to King Solomon's words, but let us take a look at the words God, Himself, spoke to the children of Israel, He said,

I call heaven and earth to witness this day against you that I have set before you life and death, the blessings, and the curses; therefore choose life, that you and your descendants may live (Deuteronomy 30:19 AMP).

Do you see the pattern in both Scriptures? First, there are only two options; and secondly, *we* do the choosing.

Option # 1 - Death through poisoning or death through the curses.

Option # 2 - Life through the logos word or life through the blessings.

Now, let me present this question to you, *"How is a blessing or curse activated?"* If you said through *speaking*, then you are correct! A blessing in the Scriptures was always pronounced by God or through His chosen king, prophet or priest. Blessings were also pronounced by fathers over their children. In the very same way, curses were activated by the *speaking* of words through the appointed authority. Do you recognize that, even today, blessings and curses still happen the same way? Many people believe, and I must also say, I have always believed that the blessings in life have everything to do with obedience to God—and it does...but hear me out...before we can obey God, we must first hear His instructions and teachings, which consist of His words; then those words are what forms pictures in our minds that show us His love, kindness and plans for our lives. And when we receive His words, these images are formed and a belief system is established. It is out of this system that our actions and behavior follow.

The writer of Hebrews states it this way: *God said, "This is the covenant I will make with them after that time, says the Lord. I will put my laws in their hearts, and I will write them on their minds"* (Hebrews 10:16 NIV).

Many times, I failed in life because I did not value God's words, so it never really got into my heart; yet, I tried to obey the "dos and do nots" in the Bible. While I behaved well for a period, I eventually failed. In other words, I lived out of a belief system in which I could attain righteousness by outward behavior, while my heart was still corrupted; thereby, yielding corrupted fruit. I thank God that His words *did* eventually make their way into my heart, after I came to the end of myself. Now I live out of a heart that is transformed by His words!

Words kill, words give life; they're either poison or fruit— you choose (Proverbs 18:21 MSG).

Let us examine the above Scripture closely: Words kill. The method King Solomon used to describe this death is the use of "poison." According to Merriam Webster's Dictionary, the definition of poison is, *"A substance that can cause people or animals to die or to become very sick if it gets into their bodies especially by being swallowed."* When I think about poisoning, I get the picture of a slow, drawn-out, painful experience. While there may be a poison that can cause sudden death, most times, that type of poison is not readily available to the regular person. The poison that King Solomon refers to, in my mind, does not give the idea of sudden death, but a prolonged suffering; all depending on the *amount* of the substance one consumes. I'm sure by now you are starting to get an understanding of the train of thought King Solomon had when he wrote this. He was trying to tell us that the words we speak are shaping the course of our lives and they will determine if we have a wonderful long life, or if it will be a life of slow poisoning.

Isn't it also interesting that the definition of poison is through the method of swallowing a harmful substance? In the natural life, we must first hear words and those words get into us, and then those words form a belief system by which we live. Now, out of the very words we've heard, or the belief system we adapt to, we then speak out words to create our lives; in the same way the poison must be ingested...then it spreads to the rest of the body.

According to the foodsafty.gov website, there are many adverse effects associated with food poisonings alone; kidney failure, chronic arthritis, brain and nerve damage and even death. Just imagine, in the natural realm, how intense and dangerous poisoning can be. But, somehow when we read the Scriptures that tell us our words can be like poison, we tend to take it so lightly; all the while ingesting poisonous words that are causing our soul (our mind, will and emotions) to become toxic, which eventually trickles over to even our bodies. The Apostle John said, *"Beloved, I pray that in every way you may succeed and prosper and be in good health [physically], just as [I know] your soul prospers [spiritually]"* (3 John 2 AMP). We cannot get away from the fact that a healthy soul leads to a healthy body—it finds its roots in the words we speak. Words are so powerful and so important, even the Apostle Peter chimed in with his take about having a good life. He stated, *"For let him who wants to enjoy life and see good days [good—whether apparent or not] keep his tongue free from evil and his lips from guile (treachery, deceit)"* (1 Peter 3:10 AMP).

I am convinced that the type of life we enjoy or endure hinges on the concept of words, first. Many folks think that if only they can get into the popular circle of highly esteemed people in society they will have a good life. Some think that if they make enough money and own a house with the fancy cars, coats, bags and shoes that life would be happy. While there is nothing wrong with all these goals and dreams, it is erroneous to think that life would be enjoyable at all times. Life may be enjoyable for a while, but when the moment passes, and reality hits, it can get pretty depressing.

Some people face a reality of knowing that all the money they had was used to overdose on drugs, or commit adultery or fornication. Some found themselves in compromising positions that caused a life-threatening disease. Many of us have failed to understand what we input to our souls has a major impact and effect on the output of our atmosphere and surroundings—that is where life or death, failure or success, disease or health, lack or abundance all lies. Imagine that for all the years you have lived on the earth, even though you might have been investing in your studies, careers, family life, business, and future that your words are the biggest and most important part of your plans. Can you imagine that up to this point you have shaped your world by the many *words* you have sent out ahead of you? Can you imagine that all this time, even though you've been equipping yourself for success, that *you* were the very one sabotaging your future? Now don't get me wrong here, I am not saying that you are a failure in any way; as a matter of fact, you might have done pretty good for yourself. But I want to stir you to think with me for a moment, could it be possible that you could have been further ahead in life, had it not been for the misuse of the power you hold with your words?

I don't want to sound like this is only bad news, because it is not, and I will get to the good news, but we must first lay the foundation on which to build the good news. I have found that when I know both sides of the story, I tend to make a better decision or choice. In today's world, everything is rushed and senses are driven—do what we feel, act how we feel and say what we feel...it's this form of living that leads to death. Here is how the Apostle Paul describes it:

For those who are according to the flesh and are controlled by its unholy desires set their minds on and pursue those things which gratify the flesh, but those who are according to the Spirit and are controlled by the desires of the Spirit set their minds on and seek those things which gratify the [Holy] Spirit. Now the mind of the flesh [which is sense and reason without the Holy Spirit] is death [death that comprises all the miseries arising from sin, both here and hereafter]. But the mind of the [Holy] Spirit is life and [soul] peace [both now and forever] (Romans 8:5-6 AMP).

We cannot escape the fact that life without the "Holy Spirit" and "Christ" *words* is a recipe for disaster. But wherever the Holy Spirit is, there will always be life. The reason I am so passionate about this topic of **words** is because most of my life I sabotaged myself and undermined the work of the Holy Spirit because of my ignorance of the power that I possessed, when I came to life with Jesus.

While I do not want to give much credence to the devil and his works, we must not continue to be ignorant of the fact that we *do* have an enemy. In all of my teachings and writings, you will hear me reiterate this point because if you don't know or believe you have an enemy of your soul, how on earth are you going to walk in victory in your health, finances, relationships, and even holiness? We need to understand that the enemy we have is already defeated, and his hopes and desires are to keep believers in the dark about their access to Jesus' power. If he can keep us blinded with a lack of knowledge, then he knows we won't be able to enforce our victory position. If this understanding of us having an enemy was not important, I don't think the Apostle Paul would have mentioned it; but he did, here is what he said, *"Lest Satan should take advantage of us; for we are not ignorant of his devices"* (2 Corinthians 2:11 NKJV). In his same letter to the church in Corinth, again, Paul talks about blindness. Let us take a look at what he said, *"The god of this age has blinded the minds of unbelievers, so that they cannot see the light of the gospel that displays the glory of Christ, who is the image of God, should shine on them"* (2 Corinthians 4:4 NKJV). The enemy thrives on God's children remaining in the dark; but I do thank God for the many ministers that are rising to bring truth to God's people. What I am trying to get across to you is that every bit of information you take in is creating a thought pattern or a belief system, and this system, in turn, will dictate the words you speak on a daily basis.

I am very thankful for Proverbs 18:21 and Deuteronomy 30:19 because, in those Scriptures, King Solomon and God offer us the option to *choose*. In fact, God did not just give the children of Israel the option to choose, but He even went a step further and told them which is the best choice; and He did that because of His love for them. God will never force us to choose, but He most definitely do His best to show us the right path. Just imagine what our lives would be like if words only had the negative effect on us or if we only had curses assigned to us. Life would prove to be very hopeless, discouraging and stressful, if we were left with the negatives alone. I am very grateful for the options that God has placed before us, and I am more grateful for His guidance and the hope that is infused in His Word. Today you have a choice: life or death, blessing or cursing, both options hinge heavily on the words you speak. And though many words have gone out in the past over your life, I want you to know it is not too late to make a change in the way you speak. My deepest heartfelt prayer is that you would ponder and meditate on the options I have laid out before you—life and death, through speaking, and my hopes is that you will make the right choice and choose life!

Prayer of Creative Words

Father, today I understand where the real power lies, and it is not in how much I own, my status or my position in society, but the real power lies in the tongue. With this understanding, I decree and declare a change in my speaking pattern.

Father, in the book of Deuteronomy You gave two options: blessings and cursing...life and death, and you suggested that I choose blessings and life. Today, I choose to speak the blessings of God, and from this release of blessings, I will walk out in the abundant life. I declare no more death words—I refuse to poison my life. Today, I say no more death words.

Holy Spirit, I ask You to give me a gentle reminder, whenever I shift off the path of life, by being tempted to speak negative words. Give me the strength to stay on the course of life by continuously aligning my words with Your words.

Father, today I stand in my position as a child of Yours, and I decree and declare that I will not remain in darkness and ignorance by the god of this age but that the light of Your Word will penetrate and decimate any form of darkness in my life.

Father, I decree and declare that my words will have its roots in Your Promises; as I speak them today, I will produce good fruit, and abundant fruit, that will not only change my life, but also others around me in Jesus name. Amen!

Chapter 3

The Tongue is Small, but Most Powerful

Even so the tongue is a little member, and it can boast of great things. See how much wood or how great a forest a tiny spark can set ablaze! And the tongue is a fire. [The tongue is a] world of wickedness set among our members, contaminating and depraving the whole body and setting on fire the wheel of birth (the cycle of man's nature), being itself ignited by hell (Gehenna). For every kind of beast and bird, of reptile and sea animal, can be tamed and has been tamed by human genius (nature). But the human tongue can be tamed by no man. It is a restless (undisciplined, irreconcilable) evil, full of deadly poison. With it we bless the Lord and Father, and with it we curse men who were made in God's likeness! Out of the same mouth come forth blessing and cursing. These things, my brethren, ought not to be so (James 3:6-10 AMP).

The above Scripture is a very intense description of the tongue. Most of us don't realize how powerful that part of our body is. The Apostle James calls the tongue a "little" member, yet he associates it with such "epic" destruction. When I look back on my life, I can remember so many scenes where the most hurt I felt and the most hurt I inflicted was through words. As a child growing up in school, there was a saying that I repeated many times out loud, whenever someone said something hurtful to me...it went something like this, "Sticks and stones may break my bones, but words will never hurt me." Unfortunately, it did not matter how loud I screamed those words...*inside* it hurt. Many of us today are still screaming those words at the top of our lungs, but we are still hurt, still bitter and still angry because the truth is that words hurt the most.

I remember recovering very quickly from a spanking from my mom; in fact, within hours, sometimes I would seem to forget that physical pain...but it took me years to recover from words spoken over my life as a child. Words like, "You are stupid" or "You will never amount to anything" or "You will always be poor and dumb" or "You are ugly." Seems too simple, but the damage was great, and so it takes years and years, sometimes, to peel away the layers of hurt and pain of misplaced words in life. We will look at how words can be used to heal your past in a later chapter, but for now, I want to establish the point that words *do* hurt, words *do* cause major damage, and words, once they are sent out, will produce something—be it good or bad.

A Word to Parents, Teachers and Leaders

If you are a parent, a teacher or a leader reading this book, I want to take some time here to appeal to you to be careful with the words you speak over the children God has placed under your care. As a reminder, children do not have less feeling because they are small, they feel the same way we do as adults, and they feel every hurtful word we speak over them. In fact, they tend to remember the hurt more as a child, and then they carry those words into their future; and that shapes their outlook on life. We must remind ourselves that we have to be good stewards over the next generation. I can also remember being pregnant and feeling the reaction from my babies in my belly by a kick sometimes while talking to him and her. As early as in the womb, you can affect your child with your words; it is a very powerful thought to think that while your baby is still in the belly they can know and feel love or rejection by simply hearing your words. Don't take this lightly, we have had too many children coming into the world fatherless and feeling unwanted and rejected. I think it is time to break that cycle and set in motion the power and authority of the creative spoken word over our children again. More than anyone else, you can influence your children to be all they can be and live out their God-purpose by just activating the words of God over them. While many people have lived life through many struggles and the harmful effects of hurtful words, many have also victoriously pressed through all the obstacles and succeeded. On the other hand, there are countless others who had parents, teachers and leaders that understood the value and power of their words over their children and their words set an easier course for their kids to make it in life. While our children will need to have their experiences in life, let us make an extra effort to help our children along the way. One of the most significant things I have noticed in the Word of God, and among the Jewish people, is the pronouncing of blessings upon their children; their words were so powerful that it would set the course of that child's life. It is my heartfelt prayer that we as parents, teachers and leaders we will get that in our spirits and start blessing our children rather than cursing them. Here is an example of the blessing Isaac pronounced over Jacob,

Then his father Isaac said, Come near and kiss me, my son. So he came near and kissed him; and [Isaac] smelled his clothing and blessed him and said, The scent of my son is like the odor of a field which the Lord has blessed. And may God give you of the dew of the heavens and of the fatness of the earth and abundance of grain and [new] wine; Let peoples serve you and nations bow down to you; be master over your brothers, and let your mother's sons bow down to you. Let everyone be cursed who curses you and favored with blessings who blesses you (Genesis 27:26-29 AMP).

Mind you Jacob did have to use trickery to get this blessing but I believe it was because he understood the power of the father's blessings, and in reading that blessing above I think I would have fought to get that as well, wouldn't you? Oh, how the enemy has stepped into our speaking, and we have caused so much damage, and we have not been aware of this cycle. My parents' generation did not have the teaching we have now, and they just did the best they knew, they followed what they saw their parents did and perpetuated the cycle of negative words. God alone knows the words that were spoken over their lives and the abundance of hurts they have carried. I am so thankful that we in this generation have a chance to reverse that, and I am praying for pastors and teachers to arise with strong conviction to set God's people free by empowering them to speak God's word. May we be enveloped again in a time when our children will run to us to be blessed! I encourage you today, even now, go to your kids if they are around and just lay your hands on their heads and speak a blessing over them. Use the same blessing Isaac spoke over Jacob and by simply doing this you would put in motion a new cycle for your children and the next generation. Parents, teachers and leaders, please take up the challenge to speak words of blessings and affirmation over your children daily, much time might be gone in your life, but it is never too late to send words out over the future generation now.

The Tongue is the Key to Controlling the Body

When we look around us or even if we were just to examine ourselves, I am sure there are some areas in our lives or should I say in our bodies that seem to rule us and no matter how hard we try we seem to be defeated in that area. I know as for me one of my weak areas is food. Oh, growing up in the Caribbean food was just a beautiful part of life. Everything is freshly grown sometimes in your home garden and if not your garden you could easily go to the neighbor's, and as a result of this freedom and unified living there was always easy access to ingredients for cooking. The food in the Caribbean is so flavorful and tasty; lots of spices and seasonings which always make food taste a whole lot better. Now do you see the power of words; just my description of the Caribbean food has set some of you to thinking about what's for dinner? Words are so powerful but back to my original point, the many weaknesses that plague us are usually fed by our physical senses. While my weakness is food, there are many different areas of life that people struggle with, for example, laziness, alcoholism, pornography, lust, greed, overeating, overspending, anger, rage, hate, bitterness, unforgiveness, lying and jealousy. I don't know what you might be struggling with or giving into, but I know we are all subject to a struggle in whatever form it takes on. I know you might be wondering what the tongue has to do with my weaknesses. Well, it has everything to do with your tongue! Let us take a closer look at what the Apostle James said, *"For we all often stumble and fall and offend in many things. And if anyone does not offend in speech [never says the wrong things], he is a fully developed character and a perfect man, able to control his whole body and to curb his entire nature"* (James 3:2 AMP).

I also want to bring this verse to you from the New King James Version; it says, *"For we all stumble in many things. If anyone does not stumble in word, he is a perfect man, able also to bridle the whole body"* (James 3:2 NKJV).

From this Scripture, you can see that the tongue that is used to speak words has everything to do with controlling the body. What I want you to pay attention to is the statement, *"If anyone does not stumble in word."* Here again the same word, *logos*, is used—the "expression of thoughts" mentioned in Chapter 1. It's the same expression of thought that God used, through the Spirit, when He created the heavens and earth. So, clearly, James is saying that when we learn to master the art of expressing our thoughts through the Spirit, we would be on the road to perfecting our lives in every area. We would be dominating our bodies, instead of it dominating us, and we will no longer be giving into every sensual desire, but we would be learning how to curb, and eventually control, that corrupt, sinful nature. I also want to point out here, the next part of the statement, "He is a perfect man." The word, "perfect", translated in the English New Testament is the Greek word *teleios*.

Strong's Concordance says that *teleios* mean "perfect; complete in all its parts, full grown, of full age, and especially of the completeness of Christian character." When James' description and Strong's definition of the word "perfect" are combined, it would read something like this, "Anyone that masters the (logos)—speaking or expressing through the Spirit of God will become perfect, have control in every area and be mature especially in Christian character." I just think that this definition is profound and mind-boggling, all at the same time. I hope you are as excited as I am because it is only when this truth is realized in our daily walk of life that will we be fully mature.

For a long time in my life, I thought if I could just practice good behavior and I would be a little closer to God, but self-will can only sustain us to a point, and then we find ourselves back to the drawing board. The Apostle James is telling us here, also, that we can identify a mature person by their speech, and I believe that now.

Let us just reason this a little further with real life, have you ever come across a mature looking person? I mean a person well dressed, maybe in his or her suit... every hair in place, they smell great, they look like a mature age, they are just well put together; and then they open their mouth, and all of a sudden, the perfection of the outward look jumped right out the door? I have had that happen to me many times, and it was totally disappointing. It appalls me to see and hear grown people using foul language in their conversations, or the demeaning way men speak about women when they get together. And this is not limited to men—women, most of the time, when they get together, they find their comfort in discussing other women's faults and shortcomings; in other words, gossiping! A person who is walking with the Lord and has some understanding of the power of the tongue can quickly identify an immature person, simply by listening to the words that's coming out of their mouths.

I've heard people say, "I just can't figure out that person." And trust me, I have used that statement many times—I think in an attempt to remain relevant and be accepted, we tend to stay around folks that are immature in their speech. Sometimes, we just don't want to lose relationships because it is all we have known our whole lives. But I want you to know that if you are ever going to mature and grow in your walk with God, there must come a time when you take stock of your words and the company you are keeping.

Look at what the Apostle Paul says, *"When I was a child, I talked like a child, I thought like a child, I reasoned like a child; now that I have become a man, I am done with childish ways and have put them aside"* (1 Corinthians 13:11 AMPC). Look closely at the order and pattern of the way we function as human beings according to Paul:

Step #1 - Speech,—"I talked like a child."
(1 Corinthians 13:11a)

Step # 2 - Thoughts —"I thought like a child."
(1 Corinthians 13:11b)

Step # 3 - Choices—"I reasoned like a child."
(1 Corinthians 13:11c)

The above pattern is pretty much the cycle that drives our lives; I used to believe that everything began with thoughts...but I must state this principle again, because so many of us have missed it: The truth is that you cannot have thoughts, unless you first hear words. The words you hear form pictures or images in your mind and become what you think about. What "you think about *you*" will be expressed through words and finally your words will create the outcome. Paul goes on to say, *"Now that I have become a man, I am done with childish ways and have put them aside"* 1 Corinthians 13:11 (AMP). He is expressing that once you have decided to mature in your walk with Christ, the first thing you have to change is the way you speak, and that my friends will change the whole cycle of thoughts and choices, thereafter. In other words, everything in our lives hinges on words! A perfect person is not someone that has no flaws, but a perfect person, according to the Bible, is one that is mature in speech because they understand that speaking by the Spirit will create God thoughts and the God thoughts will, in turn, result in mature choices.

No Human Can Tame the Tongue

The Apostle James also said, *"But the human tongue can be tamed by no man. It is a restless (undisciplined, irreconcilable) evil, full of deadly poison"* (James 3:8 (AMP). At first glance, that statement seems like really bad news, but if you look beneath the surface, it reiterates that our only hope is speaking the logos—speaking and expressing by the Spirit! No human can tame the tongue, but the Holy Spirit can, if we yield to Him. It is a very important principle to grasp because we always hear about positive thinking that will result in positive speaking. But, I present to you that if no man can tame the tongue, and only God can, then how can positive thinking and speaking have any long term lasting effect, if it is not inspired by the Holy Spirit. Notice, I did not say it won't have a positive effect, because it will; but a lasting effect is questionable. James describes the tongue as restless, undisciplined and irreconcilable (James 3:7-10 AMPC). And then he went on further to say, "*With it we bless the Lord and Father, and with it we curse men who were made in God's likeness! Out of the same mouth come forth blessing and cursing. These things, my brethren, ought not to be so*" (James 3:9-10 AMPC). It then stands to reason that if our speech never comes under the influence of the Holy Spirit, our speaking will always remain in contradiction; thereby, never producing, to the fullest capacity, because of the inconsistencies, therein, and this will result in a defeated life.

Let us look at an example of this scenario in the Bible. Most people have heard of the Apostle Peter at some point in their lives. I like to describe him as a colorful character; he was bold and brave, and I think he was very loud and boisterous, always ending up drawing all the attention to himself, when being among a crowd. He was a fisherman by trade—I am sure you have visited the fish market at some point in your life. If not, I would say "Bless God" because your ears would have been protected from some serious pollution. Peter was tough, and in my eyes, not someone that could be pushed around or bullied. He was the kind of guy that would act and then think. He never really took the time to reason things. Can you see the picture of the person

James was describing? Like in one instance, Jesus was getting ready to wash the Disciples' feet, and when it was Peter's turn, Peter threw a tantrum that in no way was Jesus going to wash his feet: *"Peter said to Him, You shall never wash my feet! Jesus answered him, Unless I wash you, you have no part with (in) Me [you have no share in companionship with Me]* (John 13:8 AMPC). Immediately, in the same breath, Peter responds, *"Simon Peter said to Him, Lord, [wash] not only my feet, but my hands and my head too"* (John 13:8 AMPC)!

In another instance, Jesus presents a question to His Disciples, *"He said to them, But who do you [yourselves] say that I am? Simon Peter replied, You are the Christ, the Son of the living God"* Matthew 16:15-16 (AMP). Of course, from the Scriptures, Jesus was shocked by the revelation Peter had, and He complimented him, He even gave new meaning to Peter's name. Jesus actually, at that moment, bestowed a blessing upon Peter. Jesus continues His conversation with the Disciples, and He talks about the impending crucifixion and the many things He will have to suffer; and guess what? Peter decides to take Jesus aside, and without thinking, rebukes him for talking that way.

But He turned and said to Peter, "Get behind Me, Satan! You are an offense to Me, for you are not mindful of the things of God, but the things of men." (Matthew 16:23 NKJV).

Do you see the pattern? James is talking about the fact that the same person can have such an awesome revelation, and yet, in the same breath, speak something evil and out of context. I want to make this point clear to you, so let us look at one more example of Peter's life...the night of the Passover. It was after the meal, Jesus took three disciples with Him to pray, in the Garden of Gethsemane, and Jesus warns them that they will all fall away from him. You guessed it!!! *"Peter replied, 'Even if all fall away on account of you, I never will.' 'Truly I tell you,' Jesus answered, 'this very night, before the rooster crows, you will disown me three times.' But Peter declared, 'Even if I have to die with you, I will never disown you.' And all the other disciples said the same* (Matthew 26:31-35 NIV). Well, the story ended where Peter *did* deny Jesus three times that night. I want you all to understand that Peter walked with Jesus for about three and a half years, and within that time, even though he was in such proximity with the Messiah, he struggled to live with consistency, and you can see this by the way he spoke. He did not know how to bridle his tongue and found himself, at times, on a mountain peak in life and the very same breath in a valley. But the key here is that the Holy Spirit was not yet given, and though Peter had Jesus' teachings, and had access to His presence, it was all still external. Peter was still operating from his own abilities; thereby, being unable to control his tongue and become mature.

Tongues of Fire

"When the day of Pentecost came, they were all together in one place. Suddenly a sound like the blowing of a violent wind came from heaven and filled the whole house where they were sitting. They saw what seemed to be tongues of fire that separated and came to rest on each of them. All of them were filled with the Holy Spirit and began to speak in other tongues as the Spirit enabled them" (Acts 2:1-4 NIV).

The day of Pentecost was a very life changing and intense day for all the Apostles and Disciples of Jesus.

He was no longer going to be with them physically, and He instructed them to gather and wait for the promise of the Father in the Upper Room. I am very sure they were anxious and probably nervous, all at the same time. The atmosphere was very tense because the persecution began to intensify, due to the leaders of that day desiring to do everything to dispel of Jesus' doctrine and deter any followers He had. The Apostles needed more than just a pep talk or positive thinking to get through the times that were ahead of them, and from the past, Peter knew he had failed, miserably. While he declared and shouted his undying loyalty to Jesus, in the same night he denies he ever knew Him. While Peter should have been watching and praying, so he wouldn't fall into temptation, he was fast asleep, and, as a result, could not control his anger. He even chopped off the ear of a solider that very night...in his desperate attempt to prove that he was strong. But then he fled the scene once fear took over.

They then found themselves waiting for a promise from Jesus because the dangerous stage they were about to embark upon in their lives could only survive on a promise. The day of Pentecost is the most beautiful and impactful scene in the birthing of the church and all of church history—the giving of the Holy Spirit! What I find most interesting is the way in which He first appears and the first thing he attaches himself to—they saw tongues of fire, and it rested on each of them, and suddenly their speech changed. Isn't it amazing that James tells us that no man can tame the tongue, and the first thing Jesus sees fit to give us is the Holy Spirit? And His priority was to infuse the tongues of the men that were afraid, men that failed miserably, men that did not live consistent with the teachings they heard, men that were not educated? My friends, while the fact remains that no human can tame the tongue, the truth of the matter is that the Holy Spirit can. Now that deserves a halleluiah right there because that tells me there is hope for you and me! Only the Spirit of God can tame our tongues, heal our speech and bring us into maturity.

Peter, the very same man who could not control his speech or his temper, the man who ran away in fear for his life because of association with Jesus, experiences the most life changing, and radical experience anyone could imagine. What happens next is astounding, there were many people from different nations in Jerusalem at that time, and many of these people spoke different languages, but the impact of what happened when the Holy Spirit came drew these visitors to inquire what was going on. They heard their native languages, and they were shocked because the Apostles were simple men, not schooled, per say, yet they were able to speak all these different languages (See Acts 2). Now, all of a sudden, with this empowering, Peter stands up to the crowd and starts speaking fearlessly, quoting the prophet, Joel, from the Old Testament to back up the experience and miracle that took place.

Then Peter stood up with the Eleven, raised his voice and addressed the crowd: "Fellow Jews and all of you who live in Jerusalem, let me explain this to you; listen carefully to what I say. These people are not drunk, as you suppose. It's only nine in the morning! No, this is what was spoken by the prophet Joel:

'In the last days, God says, I will pour out my Spirit on all people. Your sons and daughters will prophesy, your young men will see visions, your old men will dream

dreams. Even on my servants, both men and wo
will pour out my Spirit in those days, and th
prophesy I will show wonders in the heavens above
and signs on the earth below, blood and fire and bil-
lows of smoke. The sun will be turned to darkness and
the moon to blood before the coming of the great and
glorious day of the Lord. And everyone who calls on
the name of the Lord will be saved' Acts 2:14 - 21 (NIV).

On this glorious day, three thousand people got saved and were added to the church. Peter was empowered to preach, teach, perform miracles and he did it with boldness—he withstood prison and beatings. He was changed, so much, by the giving of the Holy Spirit that he even slept through the night while chained between prison guards. Peter's life is a beautiful description of how one can go from being immature to perfect, by simply yielding your tongue to the Holy Spirit and allowing Him to enable you to speak; and as you do this, everything about your life will change. You see, once you start speaking by the inspiration of the Holy Spirit, it means your thoughts and belief system will line up with the God thoughts. In other words, once you yield to the Holy Spirit, you will then begin to speak and express thoughts by His power; thereby causing lasting change. I challenge you today to ask the Holy Spirit to help you; He is only a request away!

Prayer of Creative Words

Father, today I have come to the understanding that my tongue is small and if not managed by the Holy Spirit can cause much destruction. I do not desire to cause harm or destruction to my life, so I am yielding my tongue to You. Please take control of the words I speak.

Father, today I also have come to understand that I hold the power to bless or curse my loved ones. With this knowledge, I refuse to use my words to curse; instead, I will release blessings over my husband, my wife, my children, my brothers, my sisters, my friends, my employees and my co-workers.

Father, Your Word describes a mature person as being one that speaks no idle words, and I truly desire to come into maturity—I know a true sign of maturity is manifested in speech. Holy Spirit lead me to the words of Jesus, in the Bible, and open up the Scriptures to me so that I may be able to speak life and blessings today.

Father, as I begin to read Your Word, let these words change my thoughts from negative and dark to thoughts of life and light. Paint new images and pictures from Your Word in my mind, so that I can be empowered to express your thoughts through the Holy Spirit. Help me to perpetuate life.

Father, today I decree and declare that I will put away childish speech, childish thoughts, and childish choices and I will walk out in perfection in Jesus' name, Amen!

Chapter 4

Words Can Heal the Past

We all have a past, and in the world we live in, I wish I could say that everyone experiences a past full of wonderful memories with pictures of rainbows and roses or sparkles and unicorns. Unfortunately, this is not the majority of people's past. I have found that the majority of the present plagues in life find their roots in the past and so many are unable to let go of it. One of the major weapons of the enemy is to use our past negative experiences to hinder the present and the future. I know it is very difficult, at times, when you have had major pain, abuse and hurts inflicted on you and you struggle to move forward; but, unless you get past "the past," you will be stunted in your growth, limited in your purpose, and you will sabotage your destiny. Refusal to deal with the past can cause major delays in life, and not only delays, but many dreams, goals and relationships can be aborted. I have learned that in order to change my life, I must first change my mind *about* my life. As I have been mentioning throughout this book, our thought patterns pretty much dictate our speech and our speech create the world around us. While I am fulfilling my God-purpose *now* in life, as I look back on the years, I realize

51

I could have been further in life...had I dealt with my *past* promptly!

There are many hindrances to healing the past, but I can share with you from my own experiences. I found the one hindrance I faced was rejection, and I believe every one of us has experienced rejection at some point in our lives; perhaps it's rejection of a parent, a spouse, a boyfriend or girlfriend, peers or teachers and so on. My rejection stemmed from being born out of wedlock to an inter-racial couple, and from chats with my mom as an adult, where she admitted that the option of abortion was presented to her when she was pregnant with me. So, from the womb, I received the spirit of rejection, and then my father walked out on us while I was still a baby. Having no memories of him, no picture of his facial features, his loving arms around me, no words of affirmation or guidance only surmounted the rejection. Today I don't blame him or anyone else, but I wasn't always this way. I went through years of mental torment and insecurities of never being good enough, all the while pretending I was confident on the outside. My so-called confidence was expressed by a very aggressive, foul mouthed little girl. I would present this aggressive persona around my peers, but once I got to being alone I hated myself and what I was becoming.

The spirit of rejection then gave way to independence and the goal to prove that I did not need anyone in life; my vision entailed me, myself and I, and I was determined to prove that to the world. Well, I can tell you that determination led me to many dead-end situations and enormous devastation...emotionally, physically, mentally and spiritually; but, still the need and deep-seated desire to never be rejected, again, was still the priority in my life. Independence made way for the spirit of pride, and I became unteachable and obnoxious, thinking I knew it all—I never sought advice or asked for anyone's opinions on my decisions. Oh, and did I mention that all the while I was very active in church! Yes, very active! If you never come to the point in your life where you see the need to address your past, you are on the path to being a great *pretender*.

A conscious decision of neglect to heal the past is also a conscious decision to remain superficial, and being superficial takes a lot of work, time and energy. I remember being angry at the world because of my unfortunate childhood, carrying bitterness towards people in leadership, shutting out many wonderful people because of fear of rejection. It took many life lessons to get to this point in my life and as I write these words, I don't write them for pity or from the position of being a victim. I write them so you can know that you are not alone in your suffering and affliction. I want to encourage you with my *words*—there is hope for you...just as *I* have found hope in my Savior Jesus Christ.

It was at the point of great despair that I realized that I needed help, and my pride had done a lot of damage. Let's just say, "I got real with God!" I poured out my pain and heartbreak in prayer and found myself in quiet moments, ready to hear from my Savior. One of the key verses that helped me in healing my past is, *"This Book of the Law shall not depart out of your mouth, but you shall meditate on it day and night, that you may observe and do according to all that is written in it. For then you shall make your way prosperous, and then you shall deal wisely and have good success"* (Joshua 1:8 AMP).

The above verse helped me so much that I wrote my first book, *Created on Purpose for Purpose*; around that verse, in fact, I dedicated a few chapters to just dissecting the whole process of Bible meditation. But what I want you to pay close attention to is the first line of that verse, *"This Book of the Law shall not depart out of your mouth"* (Joshua 1:8a AMP). This was the beginning of my healing. You see, unless you have something stronger and more powerful to replace the negatives in your life, it will always remain, and there is nothing more powerful and potent than God's words. His words, spoken by us, can heal any past; it matters not how far gone, or how abased, or how repulsive...once God's words are constantly being spoken...healing, restoration, and wholeness must and will come into your life. I am living proof it can be done. It is God's words that create a new picture or vision in our minds and the new pictures or visions then translate into words that we speak; thereby changing the whole trajectory of life. Isn't that great news? I know it was for me, and I also know if you would take hold of God's word, you too, can experience his healing from your past.

Ignoring is Not Forgetting

Many people want to forget the past, and that should be our ultimate goal when it comes to the negatives of our past, but there is a vast difference between ignoring the past and forgetting it. For example, a husband and wife relationship, or let's just say any relationship, be it at home, work, church or social club, as long as it involves communication with others...let's just say if an argument or disagreement should arise between a husband and wife or co-workers, it immediately opens the door to anger, discontentment and uneasiness.

Now when this happens, as humans, many times we take the position of being right, so we then tend to ignore the person, even though we have to be in the same room or space with them. But even though you are ignoring them, it doesn't mean they will magically disappear. The fact remains that when you ignore them, it doesn't mean you forget what they have said or done to you. You will notice, the more you try to ignore them, the more you find yourself thinking about the whole situation and it eventually consumes every part of you, until you can't function. You begin to feel aggravated and frustrated, not only with the person you are trying to ignore but everyone else around you. You'll find it hard to enjoy the days because the tension and stress level keeps rising. Sometimes, we think if we ignore the hurts and pains inflicted by someone it will just make life easier...because confrontation in our minds seems more difficult; but this is a trap from the enemy because if we don't confront issues in our lives, we cannot change them.

The truth is that ignoring it all may seem like the easy way out at first, but it is only a door that is left open for the enemy to enter in, fester toxic thoughts and emotions, leading us to further isolation. Having experienced this situation many times in my life, I will tell you that the only solution to deal with the issue at hand is by confronting the person and finding a solution to make things better, where both parties can resume to normal. Again, here you will see pride active, when one prefers to ignore a problem, rather than address it; which eventually leads to further complications. Prolonged ignoring of past hurts opens the door to long-term bitterness, anger issues, health problems, unforgiveness, and even hatred. My friends, it is the very

vay with the past, you can only forget the past
e the hurts of the past by dealing with it through
the lens of God's Word and not ignoring it. God's Word
doesn't erase your memory of the past, but His Word
erases the hurt associated with the past. You will never
be able to forget everything that impacted your life in
a negative way, but I can assure you, you will be able
to move forward when you address it with God's help.
Another key verse that helped me heal my broken past
is, "*But one thing I do [it is my one aspiration]: forgetting
what lies behind and straining forward to what lies
ahead, I press on toward the goal to win the [supreme
and heavenly] prize to which God in Christ Jesus is call-
ing us upward*" (Philippians 3:11a-14 AMP).

I could only have forgotten my past by first getting
God's words in my mind, forming new images of the
beautiful future He had for me; and His words enabled
me to let the pain go and take hold of the better future
in Him. So often we throw around the statement that
God's Word is powerful, but I think that is as far as it
goes; most often we never see a full manifestation of
God's Word at work in our lives. We desperately need a
revelation of the Scripture that says,

*For the Word that God speaks is alive and full of power
[making it active, operative, energizing, and effective];
it is sharper than any two-edged sword, penetrating to
the dividing line of the breath of life (soul) and [the im-
mortal] spirit, and of joints and marrow [of the deepest
parts of our nature], exposing and sifting and analyzing
and judging the very thoughts and purposes of the
heart* (Hebrews 4:12 AMP).

Can you see, from this Scripture, why the enemy
has infiltrated our words and even uses other people's

words to distort lives and destroy our destinies? While I explained from my experience that the spirit of rejection afflicted my life, the rejection was the door opener, or the root, that caused the spoken negative words of loved ones and people in authority to drive me further into despair, which was until the Word of God became a revelation to my soul and set me free. Most people today are still being affected by words that were spoken over their lives as children; because again, words shape our thoughts and our thoughts then become words.

Words of rejection, spoken over me, caused me to have a distorted life view; my view further shaped a negative world; in the same way, I am sure that many people like me have had many different types of hurtful statements spoken over them. Words like, "You are so stupid.", "You are so fat.", "You are so ugly." Or, "You are just like your father.", "You are just like your mother.", "You will never amount to anything in life." Or, "You drain me.", "You irritate me.", "Why can't you be like your sister or brother?" Or, "I can't wait for you to leave my house!", "I wish I never had you.", "You were the biggest mistake I've ever made in my life." Such hurtful words, spoken over lives, are just a few that the enemy uses. Even as you are reading this book, right now, I am very sure that even you can recall words spoken over your life that affects you until this day. Well, the good news is that God's Word is powerful, active, energizing and effective so you can start today to use God's Word to heal your past. Let me give you a statement from Scripture that helped me deal with rejection, *"I will praise You, for I am fearfully and wonderfully made; Marvelous are Your works, And that my soul knows very well"* (Psalm 139:14 NKJV). I must have spoken this Scripture a thousand times over myself, until I received the freedom from thoughts that told me I was not wanted. Notice the number of times I spoke that Scripture to myself. I had to speak it until I believed it, and I want you to know that God's Word took effect in my life. God's Word changed the way I saw myself, and in turn, the way others saw me. Because of the power of God's words, I shout with the story of my life—I'm no more rejected, but accepted, by the most important being in the universe, my Creator. I tell you, when you get free from negative words and opinions, and you replace them with God's words, there will be no stopping you in fulfilling God's purposes and plans for your life. Who would have ever thought that, today, I would be on my second book, giving advice, preaching and teaching God's Word to bring healing? I know for me, at times, it is mind boggling what God has done, and I write to tell you that if He did it for me, He most definitely can, and will, do it for you! I want to encourage you to start the healing process today, by searching out God's Word about what He has said about you— reverse the curse and change the course of your life...it is *never* too late.

Adam Heals His Past by Speaking Life Words into His Future

Let me show you, from Scripture, that after the most tragic scenario in history, that affected all humanity, how Adam did not let it deter him from moving forward. I know Adam and Eve have taken on a bad rap, and rightfully so, but I have to say that I still have much admiration for them—they paid a huge price for their mistake, but they still moved on in life; it wasn't easy, but they moved on never-the-less. Most people are very familiar with the story of Adam and Eve in the Garden—their reputation is notorious for epic failure. The Bible tells us that they entertained a conversation with the serpent (Satan) and, as a result of the conversation, acted in disobedience to God. They ate the fruit that God told them not to eat. After this act, God came walking in the Garden, as he usually did, but could not find them; God called out to them, which then started a very fearful, confrontational and judgmental conversation. God confronted Adam about his actions, and Adam started to blame God indirectly—look at his response, *"And the man said, The woman whom You gave to be with me—she gave me [fruit] from the tree, and I ate"* (Genesis 3:12 AMP). God then confronts the woman, and instead of her taking responsibility, she blames the serpent. From this pattern shown here, most often, this is how we choose to deal with our past and our mistakes. It always seems easier to blame someone else because then we never have to face and deal with the issues. While the truth remains that other people do inflict and cause pain in our lives, it cripples us from moving forward when we choose to stay in the blame game.

God immediately goes into judgment mode, and He starts to pronounce His judgment for the act of sin. Notice, God's judgment came in the form of words! *"And the Lord God said to the serpent, Because you have done this, you are cursed above all [domestic] animals and above every [wild] living thing of the field; upon your belly you shall go, and you shall eat dust [and what it contains] all the days of your life. And I will put enmity between you and the woman, and between your offspring and her Offspring; He will bruise* and tread your head underfoot, and you will lie in wait and bruise His heel. To the woman He said, I will greatly multiply your grief and your suffering in pregnancy and the pangs of childbearing; with spasms of distress you will bring forth children. Yet your desire and craving will be for your husband, and he will rule over you. And to Adam He said, Because you have listened and given heed to the voice of your wife and have eaten of the tree of which I commanded you, saying, You shall not eat of it, the ground is under a curse because of you; in sorrow and toil shall you eat [of the fruits] of it all the days of your life. Thorns also and thistles shall it bring forth for you, and you shall eat the plants of the field. In the sweat of your face shall you eat bread until you return to the ground, for out of it you were taken; for dust you are and to dust you shall return (Genesis 3:14-19 AMP).

From the Scriptures, one would reason that things would not be good from here on, and personally I would have been devastated knowing I disappointed God in such a huge way, messing up such a good thing and I am sure you would have felt the same way. Immediately we probably would have gone into major depression knowing that everything we could have need off was provided for and was so easily accessible and now just gone in an instant. Knowing that the creator of the universe would come and commune and fellowship with us, and he would walk and talk with us so freely, sharing his hearts with us. Just the thought of no longer having this relationship would have driven us to further despair. But it is here that I had to stop and take notice of the most powerful statement Adam ever made, the Scripture tells us, "The man called his wife's name Eve [life spring], because she was the mother of

all the living" (Genesis 3:20 AMP). God never n
Eve—it was Adam who named her, and he did i
after the Fall. Why? I truly believe, at the point of God's
judgment, Adam finally realized the power of words. I
think something went off in his soul—he had a revelation that the words exchanged between his wife and
the serpent landed them in big trouble and the only
way to survive the times ahead was to infuse and correct his language from there on out. It is so amazing
that while Adam knew hardships and struggle, tiredness
and pain...death and destruction was ahead of them
at that moment he chooses a name that infused life!
He was about to heal his past by speaking life into his
future. He is much to be admired, even though so
much destruction was caused as a result of his disobedience. He pressed through and adapted to the principle of words to chart the course of the future. My
friends, we are still living in the conditions that Adam
and Eve lived in, and the ways we heal our past is by
confronting it, accepting responsibility for it and then
start speaking life into our future! God's patterns are
amazingly accurate, so it would do us a world of good
to begin following them.

Prayer of Creative Words

Father, I come to You, today, recognizing my past, and
I need your help in healing my past. I have not been
able to move forward because I have refused to deal
with my past. I have blamed everyone around me for

the hurts and pains, but today, Lord, I am confronting my past with Your help.

Father, I release everyone that has hurt me and caused me pain. I let them go, as I take hold of the future You have for me. I decree and declare today I am no longer the victim, I will no longer play the blame game, but I will now use Your words to heal my past.

Father, I have decided today that I will not ignore the problems of the past and just sweep it under the rug, but I come before Your throne, and I lay all the troubles, pains and hurts at Your feet. As I do this by faith, I know, Lord, that the pain associated with my past will become less and less each day, until I forget it completely.

Father, today I thank You for the power of Your words and like Adam and Eve I will choose to speak life words over every area of my life moving forward, my mind is healed and whole, and my emotions are stable.

Father, today I submit my will to Yours, may Your wisdom flow through my mind as I make the God choices for my life, and I thank You in advance for the life that surrounds me, in Jesus name; Amen!

Chapter 5

Words Set the Course for the Future

Obviously, when we talk about the future, we know it is something that has not happened yet or something that is yet to come to pass. One of the greatest tragedies in life is to judge the future by the present circumstances. While it *does* play a part, it does not have to set a negative outcome just because where we are in life in the present may not be all that we want it to be. But here again, the enemy has found a loophole in keeping God's children in a state of flux about the future, simply because the present is somewhat chaotic.

Let us explore some of the life scenarios people might face on a day to day basis. The reason we need to break this down is because God cares about people and wants them free, being a vessel that God has called to work in the ministry—I also love and care deeply for people. I want to extend help to you, not just in theory, but in real life issues, so you will be able to relate. I want you to know, as I write these words, God wants to set you free. God wants to give you answers and connect with you in a way, so personally, that you know beyond all doubt that He cares about you and everything you are facing in your life. And most importantly, He is in the midst of the trial, pain, hurt, and loss. Take heart my friends because no matter how far you think your situation has gone...with God *nothing* is impossible.

Maybe you are in the middle of a troubled relationship or on the brink of a divorce, and when you look into the future, it seems very discouraging and bleak. You think of the years you have invested in that relationship, and you see the endless energy it is taking just to hold things together in the present. Perhaps you all have joint accounts together, and the home you own takes the two salaries to make ends meet. The fear of moving on and not being able to live comfortably may be triggering anxiety, worry and many sleepless nights, and as the days turn into nights and nights turn into days, things seems to take a turn for the worse. Relationships are so important to our well-being, and finding yourself in the middle of a broken one can leave anyone devastated and distraught, especially if you gave your best years to that relationship. For you, the future may not seem so bright, and this outlook stems from the very present situation that surrounds you.

Perhaps you are a business owner who has struggled to build a small business. And in the middle of striving to build your business, the economy took a downturn suddenly and unexpectedly, and you have lost every bit of monies invested. You had to lay off workers; creditors are pounding down your door for payments you can't make, even finding yourself on the doorsteps of bankruptcy...mouths to feed at home, kids to educate, and personal bills of your own. The stress associated with this traumatic loss of a business venture is insurmountable and there is no one to turn to because everywhere financial agencies are closing their doors. For you, the future seems hopeless now, and the thought of starting again drains every ounce of remaining strength, you may even feel like suicide is the best choice. While this might seem extreme, you will be amazed how many people have taken their lives because they were convinced their future would never turn out good because of the present state of their lives. Quite a few celebrities come to mind as I pen these words, they took their lives because their present conditions convinced them the future would be no better.

Maybe you might be someone just diagnosed with a disease; something like cancer and it's life-threatening...your children are young and is still in such need of attention from mommy or daddy. The health cost involved for the treatments, and the mere thought of the chance that there may not even be survival, has triggered other adverse effects in your body. While I use the example of cancer, this is just one disease; the list is vast in today's world of the many chronic conditions people experience like arthritis, high blood pressure, strokes, diabetes, heart conditions and insomnia—the list can go on. I don't know what health condition you may be facing, presently, but again whatever it is it may be giving you an outlook on the future that's limiting and discouraging.

Get Hold of a Promise

I only listed just a few cases of life issues that people may face, and just to reiterate the reason I listed them, is because the present situations and circumstances can greatly affect the way we view the future. Once you understand the power of words, you can then begin to have a different perspective on the future. God spoke these words to the prophet Jeremiah, *"For I know the thoughts and plans that I have for you, says the Lord, thoughts and plans for welfare and peace and not for evil, to give you hope in your outcome"* (Jeremiah 29:11 AMP).

God's word of hope, peace and welfare, spoken to Jeremiah for the children of Israel, are so powerful, aren't they? But the context of these words is amazing, and many people have not taken time out to read this Scripture in its full context. Don't get me wrong, I love this verse, it is one of the verses that I built my whole faith foundation. But when you read the verses before verse eleven, you will understand that when God sent out these words through Jeremiah, the people of Israel was actually in bondage to the nation of Babylon; they were living in a time of great despair and hopelessness. Let us take a look at the full context of the Scripture:

Thus says the Lord of hosts, the God of Israel, to all the captives whom I have caused to be carried into exile from Jerusalem to Babylon: Build yourselves houses and dwell in them; plant gardens and eat the fruit of them. Take wives and have sons and daughters; take wives for your sons and give your daughters in marriage, that they may bear sons and daughters; multiply there, and do not be diminished. And seek (inquire for, require, and request) the peace and welfare of the city to which I have caused you to be carried away captive; and pray to the Lord for it, for in the welfare of [the city in which you live] you will have welfare. For thus says the Lord of hosts, the God of Israel: Let not your [false] prophets and your diviners who are in your midst deceive you; pay no attention and attach no significance to your dreams which you dream or to theirs, For they prophesy falsely to you in My name. I have not sent them, says the Lord. For thus says the Lord, When seventy years are completed for Babylon, I will visit you and keep My good promise to you, causing you to return to this place. For I know the thoughts and plans that I have for you, says the Lord, thoughts and plans for welfare and peace and not for evil, to give you hope in your final outcome (Jeremiah 29: 4-11 AMP).

From these Scriptures, you can see God was telling them that though their present situation wasn't the best, and we all know being taken captive can never be a great place to be in life, His plans for their future were very good. You must understand that this captivity went into motion because of the disobedience to God's command to rest the land every seven years. As a result of their blatant disregard of God's Word, and His many warnings, they ended up in this mess. God did not cause this to happen to teach them a lesson, even though one would be learned; this was a result of ignoring God ways and adapting to their own. It would stand to reason then, that this trouble of captivity was brought on by their choice, yet in the middle of such distressing circumstances we see the love and mercy of a great God offering hope by giving them the promise to hold onto through it all.

I want to encourage you, here, it does not matter how bad the situation is or how far gone it is, if you hold onto the promises of God, you are guaranteed a bright and even better future. The powerful principle God was teaching the children of Israel was that they should not judge their hopes for the future on the present restrictions and obstacles. God gave them instructions to continue to live their lives in an enjoyable manner, even though it was not perfect. I want to bring your attention to something very powerful in verse six, it states, *"Take wives and have sons and daughters; take wives for your sons and give your daughters in marriage, that they may bear sons and daughters; multiply there, and do not be diminished"* (Jeremiah 29:6 AMP). Our God is always about moving forward, expanding and growing, while the enemy loves to keep us down and depressed and small in our thinking. God knew the circumstances surrounding the captives in Babylon could drive them into despair and depression. He understood that they could be tempted to give up and give in, and with that knowledge He gave them a promise. He gave them hope that the future would be great so too He doesn't want you to stop living, don't diminish just because problems arise but He wants you to keep your eyes on the promise of a great future. For example, if you are going through a divorce or separation, while that can be very difficult emotionally, please don't think that it is the end; but rather take hold of this very promise God gave the captives and activate it in your life. Speak the promise to yourself daily; remind yourself that this is not final because God has a good plan for your future. As you practice to speak the promise of the good plan, you will find that every day will get a little easier because now your focus in not on the *pain* but the *plan* that God has for your life. And like the captives, you will find the courage to live again. Maybe the extra time you now have because of fewer commitments can be used to do things that you never had the chance to do before...like travel and explore another country; perhaps go to the gym, enjoy a movie with some friends or just stack up on good books and read, peruse and further your studies or just dream again. This principle of speaking God's promise of a bright future will change your perspective of the present thereby giving hope in the midst of all the uncertainties that may surround you. Get hold of a promise because God has made many to you as His child.

Speak the Promise

Speaking a promise from God over your life can prove to be the most powerful solution to bring about change. Many times, we all want a more complex or more technical strategy for change, rather than speaking because, after all, speaking seems so easy and so insignificant. By now I'm praying that the revelation of the power of your words is beginning to sink deep into your spirit. Not only did a promise help the children of Israel while in captivity to carry on, but I want you to see that speaking that promise over your life is very, very important in how your future will turn out.

There is a story in the Bible that is most intriguing and fascinating to me. In fact, a book was written on this particular character I'm about to tell you of. The book is called the *The Prayer of Jabez*, by Bruce Wilkinson and has sold millions of copies since it was published in 2002. I remember using this prayer for a period in my life, but at the time I did not have any major revelation of the power of words. I, too, was looking for a quick fix to my life's problems without really wanting to go through the process. I did not really want an intimate relationship with Christ; I guess you could say I wanted the blessing, but not the One who gave the blessings, and, as a result, I never saw any of those words manifest in my life during that season. Your words are very powerful and they become even more powerful when they are spoken from a position of being in Christ.

Let us go back to this man named Jabez, in the book of 1 Chronicles, the first portion of the book is dedicated to listing the genealogy and descendants all the way from Adam, Abraham and then down the line to the twelve sons of Jacob (Israel). While it seems like the least interesting chapters to read, smack dab in the middle of this long list of names, in chapter four, there are just two verses that seem to jump out at you as you are reading it. At first it makes no sense as to why this is so, but as you learn to let the Holy Spirit help you in your reading of the Word you start to see an explosion of light in these two verses. Let us look at what it says,

...and Koz begot Anub, Zobebah, and the families of Aharhel the son of Harum. Now Jabez was more honorable than his brothers, and his mother called his name Jabez saying, "Because I bore him in pain."And Jabez called on the God of Israel saying, "Oh, that You would bless me indeed, and enlarge my territory, that Your hand would be with me, and that You would keep me from evil, that I may not cause pain!" So God granted him what he requested. Chelub the brother of Shuhah begot Mehir, who was the father of Eshton 1 Chronicles 4:8-11 (NKJV).

As you can see, I listed four verses for you because I want to bring to light the fact that the two verses we are looking at are sandwiched between a list of names. It is almost as if the Holy Spirit just wanted to grab hold of our attention because therein lies a very powerful and significant principle, by which God has established for us to change the course of our lives.

Here we see a young man standing out in spite of the obscurity that was associated with his name. You must understand that a name is very important in the Jewish culture; in fact, not only in the Jewish culture, but even today, having a good name, is very important in how people view us and treat us. But for the Jewish people, names were very significant and carried a lot of weight in the destiny of a child. Clearly Jabez' mother took that very lightly when she named him—she was not thinking about the implications or obstacles that would stand in her son's way, but she was rather focused on what she was going through at the time and in turn projected that onto her son. She did not understand the power of her words, because in naming her son, she attached a curse that would be perpetuated for the rest of his life—everyone that would call Jabez' name would, in fact, be releasing a negative prophetic statement over his life. Look again at what she said, *"And his mother called his name Jabez saying, "Because I bore him in pain"* (1 Chronicles 4:9b (NKJV). To me, this is very heartbreaking, especially now that I have understood the power of *my* words. And many of us might stop and think to ourselves this is so cruel, yet we fall into the same trap today; we may not name our children negative meaning names, but the words that we release over them can make or break them.

Can you imagine for a moment, every time Jabez heard his name, the words, *"You cause pain!"* would echo in his ears, the fact of knowing what his mother was feeling when she bore him was a constant reminder in his soul. I cannot begin to imagine it, and I probably would have walked out that prophecy by continuously causing pain to others. In the midst of this tragic scenario, the Bible describes this young man as being more honorable than his brothers. I truly believe Jabez had a revelation about the God he served, and as a result, that revelation led him to understand the power of words. He was able to recognize that he did not have to accept the fate his mother pronounced over him, but rather he could move into the realm of faith and counteract that doomed destiny. He bypassed the natural circumstances and went directly to the source of his life. I love the fact that he did not argue with God; he did not take on a victim mentality, and he did not play the blame game. He didn't even ask God to change his name. Jabez did not tell God all about his problems, but he spoke specifics to counteract that which was assigned to him.

There is so much to learn from these two little verses, and I trust that we will adapt this principle in prayer. Instead of telling God all that is wrong, and complaining about people who inflicted the pain and hurt on us, we would start praying the specifics to counteract the problem, in other words, we would start praying and speaking the solution rather than the problem.

Jabez followed the same principle of speaking, just like his mother used words to pronounce the curse; he used words in prayer to pronounce the blessing and change the course of his destiny. Jabez went against every negative connotation assigned to his name. Let us look at what he said, "*And Jabez called on the God of Israel saying, "Oh, that You would bless me indeed, and enlarge my territory, that Your hand would be with me, and that You would keep me from evil, that I may not cause pain!" So God granted him what he requested* (1 Chronicles 4:10 NKJV).

First, we see that Jabez asked to be blessed because his mother associated him with pain, and we all know that pain can never be a blessing; in actuality, he was reversing the curse of pain by activating the blessings in his life.

Second, he spoke enlargement of territory because he knew he would need room to hold the blessings. He was prophesying to be able to contain the blessings that God would release into his life.

Third, he spoke God's hand to be with him; in other words, he was speaking Gods guidance for the rest of his life. When we have God's hand, not only is that provision, but that speaks of a leading...like a child putting their hand into daddy's hand for guidance and safety.

Fourth, he spoke protection, because he knew when blessings would come, he did not want to find himself abusing the blessings. But instead he would become a blessing because he also spoke in prayer that he would not cause pain.

I want you to pay attention to the fact that though his mother spoke only one statement over his life, he spoke approximately four statements to counteract that one. More and more science is proving the principles in the Bible to be true. Peggy Bert from her blog *"Positive and Negative Words"* states,

"How many positives are needed to offset one negative? At least two-to-one, experts say. Researchers have concluded that when applying this formula to our most intimate relationships, like marriage, the ratio of positives must be even higher. Among those researchers is psychologist Dr. John Gottman at the University of

Washington. Gottman says the formula should be five to one for married couples. So how do you accomplish that? Increase positives while reducing negatives. Boost the frequency of small positive acts so that the ratio reaches five-to-one."

This information is mind boggling—to think that for every negative word we release, we then need two or more positive words to undo it. And mind you, Jabez did not have this research in his time to prove this principle; yet, with the relationship he had with God and the help of the Holy Spirit through prayer. he was able to change the course of his destiny. Jabez understood the power of negative words, but he also understood the power contained in God's words to undo the damages that were set in motion.

Like Jabez, it is imperative that we become aware of the words we are speaking, because it is shaping our world—if God did it for Jabez, He can do it for us, but I believe we must establish the principle of the continuous declaration of God's word over our lives. God granted Jabez his request and I know He will grant yours; increase in speaking His word and you will decrease in speaking death words!

I want to encourage you, God knows your pain is real, the hurt is real, and He knows every hurtful word that was spoken to you; but He does not want you to remain under this painful state for too long because if you do you will begin to diminish. God is not insensitive to your struggles and pain, but as the children of Israel and Jabez, He wants you to arise and speak in faith the words to counteract the curse. And more than anything else, He wants you to know He is right there with you. Look at the words God spoke to the children of Israel,

But now, GOD's Message, the God who made you in the first place, Jacob, the One who got you started, Israel: "Don't be afraid, I've redeemed you. I've called your name. You're mine. When you're in over your head, I'll be there with you. When you're in rough waters, you will not go down. When you're between a rock and a hard place, it won't be a dead end—Because I am GOD, your personal God, The Holy of Israel, your Savior. I paid a huge price for you: all of Egypt, with rich Cush and Seba thrown in! That's how much you mean to me! That's how much I love you! I'd sell off the whole world to get you back, trade the creation just for you (Isaiah 43:1–4 MSG).

It is very important that you get hold of the Scripture above that no matter what know that God is with you. Do not allow the enemy or anyone else to convince you otherwise, because as long as you have that promise from God's word it will come to fruition in your life once you don't diminish in your speaking of that promise.

Prayer of Creative Words

Father, today I decree and declare that the present situations and circumstances I am facing will not determine my future to be a discouraging end.

Father, I decree and declare that in this present pain lies purpose for my future. I have hope that does not disappoint because my hope is based on a promise from You.

Father, today I am standing on Your promises because I know Your promises are true, and they will come to fruition in due season as I speak them out over my life.

Father, I decree and declare that I will not diminish in these difficult conditions but that my wisdom, joy, strength and confidence will now multiply as I stay connected to You and continuously speak Your words.

Father, I thank You for Your promise; You will never leave me nor forsake me, in the midst of these deep waters, this fiery furnace, and this seemingly dead end. I hold onto Your words…that the plans you have for me are good, my future looks good, and I speak and establish these words in my life.

Father, I stand on Your word that reassures me that You paid a huge price for me. If You have seen such great value in me, then I will not allow the words spoken over my life in the past to hinder me any further. I thank You for loving me, believing in me and for becoming my personal God.

Father, I want to thank you in advance for healing my life and for allowing a chance to dream again, to have new hope and now I can love again. My hope and peace are in You, and my soul finds rest from the past in you Lord.

Father, today I declare, like Jabez, that you would bless me indeed, that You would enlarge my territory so that I will be able to contain the blessings. Thank You for Your hand being upon me; please lead, guide and keep me from all evil, and may I never cause anyone pain. I send these words out today with great latitude and I know the destiny of my life is changing in Jesus name…Amen!

Chapter 6

Expect Miracles When God Asks a Question

And I answered, O Lord God, You know!"
Ezekiel 37:3 (AMP)

God presents a question to the prophet Ezekiel, but God is all knowing, so why would he need to ask a question? In general, I don't think God asks questions because he doesn't know the answer, but rather He asks questions in an attempt to get us to think and reason outside of the box of the natural—entering the realm of the kingdom, where the *impossible* becomes *possible*. He asks us questions to stretch our faith and test us about our knowledge of Him and His abilities. He asks questions so we can take stock of our relationship with Him and our belief patterns. He simply asks questions to see if we know where we are at that point in our lives. And finally, I think He asks questions *to prepare us for a miracle*.

In the book of Genesis, God's first question was presented to Adam, *"But the Lord God called to Adam and said to him, "Where are you?"* (Genesis 3:9 AMP). I don't believe that God wasn't aware of where Adam was; it was like an investigator asking interrogating questions to a suspect...in the investigator's mind, the result is pretty much known, but he has to ask questions to get the suspect to confess the truth.

As a parent, I am often on this end of asking questions to my children like the one God asks Adam. My children, and I am sure if you have children, also, you are very familiar with this type of questioning; they do something wrong and try to cover it up, but as parents we already know what they've done. For them to recognize the place they have found themselves in requires a line of questioning, rather than accusation. It is just amazing to me how God works in bringing light to our dark areas, He gives us opportunities to come and approach Him without fear as we confess the truth by the quiet convictions in our hearts as opposed to the devil who comes with condemnations and accusations that drives us to despair. God is gentle in His leading and guiding leaving us with a sense of hope and peace while the devil will always leave us feeling unworthy and hopeless.

In the New Testament, Jesus displayed his teaching style by asking many questions to the audience to get them to think and to take stock of their lives, their actions, and their belief patterns. He asked questions like, *"And which of you by worrying can add one hour to his life's span"* (Luke 12:25 AMP)? *"For what will it profit a man if he gains the whole world [wealth, fame, success], but forfeits his soul? Or what will a man give in exchange for his soul"* (Matthew 16:26 AMP)? *"You are the salt of the earth. But if the salt loses its saltiness, how can it be made salty again"* (Matthew 5:13a NIV)? *"If you love those who love you, what reward will you get? Are not even the tax collectors doing that"* (Matthew 5:46 (NIV)? *"Why do you look at the speck of sawdust in your brother's eye and pay no attention to the plank in your own eye? How can you say to your brother, 'Let me take the speck out of your eye,' when all the time there is a plank in your own eye"* Matthew 6:3-4 (NIV)? *"Which of you, if your son asks for bread, will give him a stone? Or if he asks for a fish, will give him a snake"* Matthew 7:9-10 (NIV)? *"By their fruit you will recognize them. Do people pick grapes from thornbushes, or figs from thistles"* Matthew 7:16 (NIV)? Jesus was very concerned about every area of the people lives, and his method of teaching them were very engaging. His teaching required their participation, and from His method of questions, we can see a *relationship* being His goal. He did not just hand out harsh rules, but provoked them to think, which eventually brought *change* to their lives.

Sometimes Jesus would ask a question just before he performed a miracle, and personally these are my favorite questions. For example, there was a time when Jesus was going to Jerusalem for a Jewish festival, and on His way, He passed by a gate called the Sheep Gate; there was a pool situated at this gate. Many lame, blind and physically challenged people would gather at this pool. It was told, in the story, that at a certain time of the year an angel would come down and stir the waters in the pool, and whoever made it first into the pool would receive their healing.

Well, the Bible tells us that a particular lame man had been waiting there for thirty-eight years and had never been able to get in the water on time (See John 5:1 – 5). Jesus knew this man's condition, and I am very sure he had knowledge of how long he suffered from the condition. Guess what? Yes! You guessed it...Jesus asked that man a question that transformed his life forever. Here is what the Bible says,

When Jesus saw him lying there, and knew that he already had been in that condition a long time, He said to him, "Do you want to be made well" (John 5:6 NKJV)?

Jesus listened to the man's response and then He spoke a few words of instructions to the man—as the man obeyed Jesus' words he was *instantly* healed.

On another occasion, Jesus was on His way to Jericho and, of course, there were lots of people following and surrounding him. The Bible tells us there was a blind beggar sitting by the roadside, and he heard all the commotion of the crowds. When he enquired, he was told *"Jesus of Nazareth was passing by"* (Luke 18:36 NIV). I am sure he had heard the stories of Jesus' miracles and knowing Jesus was right there he used the one thing that could draw attention to himself—his voice—his words—and he started shouting to get Jesus' attention. The crowd around him tried to keep him quiet, but he didn't give up; as a result of his persistent speaking, he caught Jesus' attention. You must know by now that a miracle was about to happen because Jesus asked him, *"What do you want me to do for you"* (Luke 18:41 NIV)? The beggar's blindness was now history because Jesus wanted to work a miracle in his life (See Luke 18: 35-42). You see, my friends, miracles can ensue from one question from God, and today He is still asking us questions like, *"Daughter do you want to be healed?"* or *"Son do you think this business can succeed?"* His questions are doorways for miracles to flow into your life, so don't run away when He asks you questions, but rather be ready to answer like the lame man and the blind beggar.

Let me share with you one more of my favorite questions that led to the miraculous...it is a question that radically transformed a terrorist's life and made him a pioneer of the early church—that question was presented to none other than the Apostle Paul.

As he traveled, he approached Damascus, and suddenly a light from heaven flashed around him [displaying the glory and majesty of Christ]; and he fell to the ground and heard a voice [from heaven] saying to him, "Saul, Saul, why are you persecuting and oppressing Me?" And Saul said, "Who are You, Lord?" And He answered, "I am Jesus whom you are persecuting, now get up and go into the city, and you will be told what you must do" (Acts 9:3-6 AMP).

The Apostle Paul was on a mission to eradicate the followers of Jesus, and it was one encounter, with one question, that changed his life so radically that he ended up dying for the cause of Christ. He received so much intimate revelation because of that one question, and we have most of the New Testament letters for instruction for Christian living because of this Apostle. His life was a miracle, and it started with one *question*.

In the same way, as your walk with the Lord grows, you will begin to recognize that God will speak to you, sometimes, through *questions*. As your faith grows, the questions will become more intense, but it's not for you to be afraid, but rather to see it as an opportunity for you to go deeper in your trust of the Lord...knowing that He wants to work miracles through those tough questions. I love it when God asks me questions because it gives me an opportunity to search out His Word, reflect, and take stock of where I am. I love His questions, also, because it gives me a sense that a miracle is around the corner, and He is getting me ready to receive it. I love God's questioning method!

Now, I did not forget Ezekiel's question, let us return to the question presented to him, but let us take it in context,

The hand of the Lord was upon me, and He brought me out in the Spirit of the Lord and set me down in the midst of the valley; and it was full of bones. And He caused me to pass round about among them, and behold, there were very many [human bones] in the open valley or plain, and behold, they were very dry. And He said to me, Son of man, can these bones live? And I answered, O Lord God, You know (Ezekiel 37:1-3 AMP)!

The prophet, Ezekiel, had a vision that was from the Lord, and in this vision he was led out into the valley of dry bones; it was not *literal* dry bones, but rather a representation of the state that the people of Israel was in at the time. God was allowing Ezekiel to see the condition of the people's strength mentally, physically and spiritually—they had lost their will to fight and were pretty much wasting away. When I think about dry bones, the idea of "no return" pops into my mind; it also gives the idea of being in that condition for a very long time. You must also use your imagination here with me to get the intensity of the decayed state of this impossible scene.

The valley is surrounded by mountains, it is low down, and this is not one person's bones in the vision; Ezekiel saw the *whole house* of Israel in this condition—piles and piles of dry bones just stacked upon each other; in my mind it seems like a scene from a futuristic movie where aliens invaded earth and kill all humans and leaves all the remains behind. I know, I have an overactive imagination, but you have to get in your spirit that this was not one skeletal lying in a ditch. So by now, I am thinking you have the picture embedded in your mind. Now let's take our imagination just a little further and dare to put ourselves in Ezekiel's shoes, let us imagine God bringing us to this scene and then presenting the question, *"Can these bones live?"* What would be your response? Well, first of all, if it were me, I would try to wake myself out of that vision immediately or in the vision I would try to find a clear path and start running for my life. I would probably go off thinking that I was going to be added to the stockpile and probably go unconscious right there on the scene. I know you are laughing at me, but I am very honest here. Let's just say I decided to stay and answer the question, I think my response would be an emphatic, *"Heavens no!"* But God dares to ask Ezekiel this and his response was amazing, he said, *"O Lord God, You know* (Ezekiel 37:3b AMP)! In essence, Ezekiel was saying, "I think you already know the answer to that one Lord, so let the miracle begin." It is a very beautiful answer from Ezekiel because it shows the level of confidence he has in God's abilities. I'm sure Ezekiel thought to himself, this is not possible, but if God sees fit to ask this question, then there has to be a way that it can be done, and he releases His trust and faith in God for the rest of the instructions.

What are *Your* Dry Bones?

Today, God may not be asking you about an army of men's dry bones, but the bones are a representation of the things you value and cherish in life like relationships, health, businesses, finances, marriage and so on, that have seemingly died on you. The truth is that God gave us these relationships and abilities and talents to make our lives better, enabling us to make a difference in this world. But, as you are well aware, by now, because I keep sounding the alarm, we have an enemy that seeks to steal kill and destroy according to John 10:10. So everything that God destines and purposes for us is always good, and once we get hold of that concept, as discussed in the previous chapter, it tends to stir up the enemy more because he knows he is losing another soul to the kingdom of God. He then moves into high gear in order to disrupt, and even try to stop, the purposes of God for our lives.

I often tell my congregation, "A person who has gotten hold of their 'God-purpose' will become a moving target for the devil." Now that explains a lot, as to why life can be tough at times. In the middle of having this enemy, God gives us the principle of speaking words that can easily combat the devices and weapons formed by the enemy and we don't have to be afraid of his tactics, we just need to be aware of them.

One thing I have also come to understand is that no matter what area of dry bones you are dealing with in your life, the principle of solving them all starts the same way—by speaking! Compared to the extremities of Ezekiel's vision your life may not be anything close to that description of dry bones, but, never-the-less, dry bones may exist in your life. A principle I use, and has have proven to be very helpful in my healing process is writing. In writing out my issues, I get a clearer picture in my mind as to the state and condition of my soul, and I want to encourage you to try it also. Everyone is not the same, but I know God's principles work, and if you want the dry bones in your life resurrected, sometimes you have to take drastic, out of the box, bold steps in the process. So, at this point, feel free to grab your journal or just some paper for writing.

God brought Ezekiel in his vision to a valley and showed him the dry bones; God caused Ezekiel to walk through the midst of the dry bones because He wanted Ezekiel to have a clear picture and assessment of the situation at hand. You see, before we can give a faith answer to God, we must first be aware of what the problem is. So, in this little time, I want you to use your journal or piece of paper and write the date...then write out the situation in your life you deem as being past the point of no return. Just like Ezekiel explained his vision, so you can see and feel the sense of being in a dark, dead and lonely place...I want you to do the same...explain your vision.

I know many people would say, "Well you don't need to focus on the problem." And they are right, you do not need to focus on the problem, but you *do* need to *identify* the problem. The reason I want you to do this is because you cannot fix what you don't identify; you cannot effectively pray the promises of God, if you have not appropriated which promises are necessary for your situation. If the "dry bones" situation in your life is sickness, and you are standing on Scripture for finances, then there will never be any manifestation of healing in your life because there is a misappropriation of the Word and that would prove to be ineffective, while you may get a financial blessing, you may remain sick in your body. Or, if you are praying for salvation for your loved ones, but standing on healing Scriptures, there again, is a misappropriation of the Word and the results won't be forthcoming. One of the major mistakes

I see in believers' lives is the unwillingness to deal with issues *specifically*; sometimes because they just don't know how to and often because they are just too lazy to seek out the steps necessary to fix them.

I have been there in my life; there were times I just did not want to deal with my issues and then there were times where I just wanted God to step in and rearrange it for me without me doing anything. I use to pray just general prayers like, "God bless my home and family", "God, You know what is in my heart, so please fix it." But there are patterns with God, and once I got teachings on His ways, my life changed completely.

King David, in one of His Psalms, said, *"He made known His ways [of righteousness and justice] to Moses, His acts to the children of Israel"* (Psalm 103:7 AMP). You can see that Moses experienced a different level in His relationship with God because he knew God's ways, not just His works.

When we learn to move past just wanting our needs met and into an intimate relationship with God, then we will learn that He has the best plans in store for us, and He wants to work miracles in our lives. My life could not have changed, until I identified my problems and made a conscious effort to know the God, who wanted to heal me and bring my dead bones back to life. My point is, if your life is going to change, and your dead bones scene is going to be resurrected, you first have to identify what the problem is, and then find the Word of God that matches your need for your speaking to become effective.

Without identification of the issues of your life, there will be no healing, freedom or victory. Now that you know *why* you need to identify the issues, I trust that you will take the necessary steps, by simply writing them

down for clarity and assessment. I can assu
once you decide to take this step of faith, y
will begin. After you have identified and wr
your valley of dry bones, I want you to write
tion, *"Can these bones live?"*; then, I want you to answer the question by writing, *"Only you know Lord!"*
With the rest of space left, I want you to leave it available, as you would need to come back to your journal,
or piece of paper and write the promise, or promises, of
God from His Word, as your daily declarations. From
here on out, while reading this book, make sure you
have your journal or piece of paper handy, because
once you are finished with the following chapters, you
will have a solid understanding of the "speaking" process and will need it as your daily companion.

Prayer of Creative Words

Father, today I want to thank You for bringing light into
my soul, and I want to thank You for the questioning
process. I will not be afraid of Your questions, but, I will
embrace them.

Father, I am open to Your questioning method because I want to take stock of my life, I want the light of
your Word to be cast upon my belief patterns, and I
want to experience Your supernatural intervention in
my life.

Father, I decree and declare that my life will be a
miracle, just like the Apostle Paul's life was, and I want
You, Lord, to present to me the question or questions
that I need in order to steer me in the direction of becoming that miracle.

Father, I will not run away anymore from the issues and dry bones in my life, but like Ezekiel, I stand in the valley trusting You in this process. Yes, I am a bit scared but I know that if You ask me a question, it is because You already know the answer, and I will follow the way You are leading in this valley.

Father, I have come to the understanding that I cannot confront, fix or change what I do not identify, and I declare that my eyes will be open and sensitive to see that which needs changing.

Father, I have decided that I will not stay focused on the dry bones around me because I know this situation is subject to change in my life, I know that if You caused the Apostle Paul's life to change, You can change *my* life.

Father, I want to identify my dry bones, and I have purposed today that I will write them down, so that I can have clear assessment. I will now find Your words, to appropriate to my issues, so that life, healing, freedom, and victory can flow into my valley, in Jesus Name, Amen!

Chapter 7

Prophesy

Now that you have been able to identify, clearly, the dry bones and what they represent, it's time to look at the solution for the problem...be it marriages, finances, health, a broken past, an addiction, abuse or whatever you have listed as your "dry bones." It's time to see the *impossible* become *possible*, as you now partner with God! After the great question is presented to Ezekiel about the bones, and Ezekiel responds in faith, the Lord then immediately moves to the instructions for what's next.

What I want you to pay close attention to is that, once you list or assess the problem, you now have to listen to the instructions from the Lord, so that you can move forward. We are not supposed to identify the problem and keep identifying the problem, but that's what we do in life, most of the time. When we have a problem of epic proportion in our lives, and someone asks us how we are doing, we immediately spew out from our mouths the problem, the pain, the hurt, the feelings of disappointments, etc. Does this sound familiar? Of course, after the fall of man, our speaking became corrupted, and instead of life words coming automatically, our wiring was shorted out and only the Word of God can fix that shortage—this is why this principle of speaking is so very important. So pay close attention to what the Lord says to Ezekiel in the next few verses,

Again He said to me, "Prophesy to these bones and say to them, O you dry bones, hear the word of the Lord. Thus says the Lord God to these bones: Behold, I will cause breath and spirit to enter you, and you shall live; And I will lay sinews upon you and bring up flesh upon you and cover you with skin, and I will put breath and spirit in you, and you [dry bones] shall live; and you shall know, understand, and realize that I am the Lord [the Sovereign Ruler, Who calls forth loyalty and obedient service]" (Ezekiel 37:4 – 6 AMP).

The first thing God tells Ezekiel after the assessment of the problem is, *"Prophesy to these bones and say to them, O you dry bones, hear the word of the Lord!"* (Ezekiel 37:4 AMP). Vine's Concise Dictionary says that prophesy means "to speak God's message under the influence of the divine spirit." Right here, from the definition of the word "prophesy," you can see the connection back to Genesis, in God's creation process, where God spoke the word of divine inspiration and everything we see today came out of that spoken word; some six thousand plus years later, the principle is still the same. What is important to understand is that you are not just speaking "positive" words. Positive words, alone, are not the full scope of prophesying; while it involves positive words, it is not limited to *just* "positive" words. There are many positive people out there in the world, but the results are still very limited to them and their will power to remain positive; but this prophesying is totally contingent on God's words, not ours. Jesus said, *"The words that I speak to you are spirit, and they are life"* (John 6:63b NKJV). I have to reiterate that our speaking must go beyond just positive words and cut straight into the realm of the kingdom and speak Jesus' words. *Why?* Why am I so adamant about this? Because I have been there, and as a Pastor, I see, hear and speak to so many people that are just desperate for a change in their lives; and they try speaking positive words, they try repetitious positive phrases that some motivational speaker introduced to them. Please do not get me wrong, I am not against motivational speakers, because they do help a lot of people; but my point to you is that if this motivation does not stem from God's words and His truths, it will be difficult to maintain. My mandate and mission are to get as many people on board to speaking the words of Jesus Christ, because from his lips to our ears he said, *"His words are spirit and life"* (John 6:63b NKJV). Here is another reason I am adamant about you speaking God's words, and not just positive words...look at what God said through his prophet Isaiah,

For as the rain comes down, and the snow from heaven, And do not return there, But water the earth, And make it bring forth and bud, That it may give seed to the sower And bread to the eater, So shall My word be that goes forth from My mouth; It shall not return to Me void, But it shall accomplish what I please, And it shall prosper in the thing for which I sent it (Isaiah 55:10-11 NKJV).

The Scripture above is most powerful and is foundational in building your relationship with Christ. God cannot lie, and I truly believe every word in the Bible is from God. God's Word never returns to Him void, and with a foundation like this, you can rest assured that when you speak His words over your life, you will see situations and circumstances begin to change.

Prophecy to Your Problems (dry bones) the Solution

The next part of the statement to Ezekiel was,

Thus says the Lord GOD to these bones: "Surely I will cause breath to enter into you, and you shall live. I will put sinews on you and bring flesh upon you, cover you with skin and put breath in you; and you shall live. Then you shall know that I am the LORD" (Ezekiel 37:5-6 AMP).

God instructed Ezekiel to prophesy the solution to the problem; he told him to speak to the bones, not his words, but God's words. Therein, lies the answer to many of our problems; instead of saying what God has said concerning us, we continue to state the problem— we rehearse the problem until the problem is all we see, feel and think. Imagine if Ezekiel was not obedient to God, and did not have a strong confidence level in his God, what would have happened? If Ezekiel was like some of us, and notice, I am included, I think the scenario and Ezekiel's speaking would sound something like, "My God, there is no way this could ever get better, there is no way these bones could ever come alive. It is only a matter of time before I get to being like these bones, this is just hopeless." Or, "Even if I go to the hardware store and buy all the glue in stock, I will never be able to stick all these bones back together. In fact, I will grow old trying to fix this, I don't even know which bone to attach to which bone; I might as well give up now and look for another and easier way out." Or, "This just might not be God's will, so why waste time trying, I am sick and tired of waiting, trusting and trying, God doesn't seem to care." Do these statements sound familiar? Of course, because this is the way we have all been speaking all of our lives about our marriages, our children, our finances and our health; but God is trying to show us that there is a different way, and it is so simple that many of us discard it because of the simplicity.

We always want something more in-depth, and more intricate, and more complicated, so that our egos can be stroked and we feel we are accomplishing something, when it's difficult. But God's ways are higher than our ways and in His Word he says, *"But God has chosen the foolish things of the world to put to shame the wise, and God has chosen the weak things of the world to put to shame the things which are mighty;"* (1 Corinthians 1:27 NKJV). God will use something as simple as words that are infused with His power to ignite life and bring change to those who will trust Him whole-heartedly. The whole essence of our speaking is not only to bring those things back to life for us, but in the midst of our situation changing, there is a dynamic at work that causes us to know beyond the shadow of a doubt that He alone is the God of the impossible. Your dry bones situation opens up a portal for God's glory to shine in, and that breeds a deeper understanding of who God is on a very personal level. I am of the opinion that without "dry bones" situations many of us would never really come to know the greatness of our God. When I look back on my life, I can never stop thanking God for the many difficult times I faced, the many dry bones situations I encountered, because truly had it not been for those times, I probably would have been out in the world and very far from God. I would not have seen the need to depend on God as I have and I probably would not be writing this book today. I am convinced that there are so many hidden potentials in you and this principle of speaking God's Word, over a period of time, will unlock that door and you will begin to see dry bones come to life. All your broken dreams, all the seemingly wasted years, all the heartbreak and depression, all the sleepless nights, anxiety and fear will begin to leave, and you will see yourself rise again so don't give up now.

I want to offer you practical help in the area of prophesying, just as God spoke to Ezekiel, and he told him what to speak to the dry bones. In the same way, the Bible holds many words or promises that apply to your situation, and I want us to look at at least one problem area in life and address it the same way Ezekiel did. It is now time to stop rehearsing the problem and start prophesying the solution. Let us look at something that might be common to us all, no matter what our backgrounds; financial issues seem to plague us all, some more than others, but I'm sure it is common to man, everywhere. Your financial problem may vary from millions or thousands of dollars in debt to just making enough to get by from month to month...with nothing left over, or even coming up short before the month is over. It matters not where you are on the scale, because to each person, this is a struggle of epic proportion. The good news is that God has said some things concerning your situation, and we need to find out what God has said about your financial standing and prosperity. Below I have pulled out promises from God's Word and laid them out for you, in the first person, so you can speak these promises as your source to prophesy over your financial breakthrough. Start prophesying today!

My Prophetic Words

Father, today I stand on Your Word and the principle of prophesying. I believe Your Word is true and never returns unto You void, or without producing that which it was sent out. With great confidence in You, Lord, I send forth these words over my financial dry bones:

I prophesy that Your divine power has given me all things that pertain to life and godliness, and I thank You that life is coming to my finances (2 Peter 1:3 NKJV).

I prophesy, my Father's will is for me to prosper and be in health, even as my soul prospers, I prophesy over my financial situation, and I declare it is turning around even now (3 John 2 AMP).

I prophesy, my Father gives me the power to get wealth, that I may establish His covenant in the earth, today as I gain wealth I will remember it comes from You, Lord (Deuteronomy 8:18 AMP).

I prophesy that because I have listened to Your Words, and have been obedient to them, Father command your blessings to come upon my finances and your blessings to overtake me now (Deuteronomy 28:2 AMP).

I prophesy that I will honor You with my capital and with the first fruits of all my income; and You promise that my storage places, my bank accounts, will be filled with plenty and my vats will overflow with new wine, new business, new ideas (Proverbs 3:9-10 AMP).

I prophesy that You can make all grace abound toward me that I always have all sufficiency in all things, and I will have abundance to overflowing (2 Corinthians 9:8 NKJV).

Father, according to Your Word, I ask you to command your blessings on me in my home, in my business, in my workplace and my finances and all that I put my hands upon (Deuteronomy 28:8 NKJV).

I prophesy, based on Your Promise, that You will open to me Your good treasure, the heavens, to give me rain on my land in its season, I prophesy this is my season of blessings and the work of my hands is prospering and yielding fruit. In this season, I will lend and will not borrow any more. (Deuteronomy 28:12 NKJV)

I prophesy today that no weapon formed against my finances, my business, my job or my education will prosper; I prophesy that all evil words and words of failure will be null and void because I am a child of God, and I walk in His righteousness (Isaiah 54:17 NKJV).

I prophesy that my mind will be constantly renewed by Your words, Lord, and not words of failure. I prophesy that I have a fresh mental and spiritual attitude Ephesians 4:23 (AMP).

I prophesy that like Caleb and Joshua, I have what it takes to possess all that God has designed for me to have and I am well able to overcome every financial obstacle. I prophesy I have an overcoming spirit (Numbers 13:30(NKJV).

I prophesy that my God shall supply all my needs according to his riches in glory by Christ Jesus. (Philippians 4:19 KJV).

All these words I send out and seal in Jesus' name, Amen!

Great job! You did an amazing job on your first attempt of prophesying according to God's Word. While the above prophetic declarations are specifically for finances, the pattern is the same for all other life issues... be it health, salvation for loved ones, marriage, relationships, fear, forgiveness, anger, etc. God has given promises for every issue we may face in life. All we have to do is have a desire to be free, and then search out His Word for the answer. Now, I want you to return to our journal or page that you had set aside in the previous chapter and follow the same pattern as above, by searching out the Promises for your situation and write out the prophetic declarations there. I know you all may not know where to look for the Scriptures that pertain to your particular issue, but the internet is a great source of help in today's world. All you need to do is type in the issue you are dealing with, for example, "Scriptures for healing", and there will be many resources that will come up; then you can choose the ones appropriate for you. Whatever the issue, you will be able to find it online and in your actual Bible. Once you have completed this, you will now be able to have a full picture of your present situation and a prophetic picture of your future. And this will show you that you don't have to remain where the problem is, but now you can break through a clear path by speaking God's Word over the problem. I would recommend that you make these prophetic declarations at least twice a day, for a month, so that you can get these words in your spirit and start altering the thought patterns that had you bound for failure. You can do it for as long as you like, but I recommend at least one month to start. I guarantee you your life will begin to change, your faith will increase and in the process you will begin to reprogram your words from death to life.

WORDS

Chapter 8

Keep Prophesying Until Life Comes

On persevering prayer: *"I look at a stone cutter hammering away at a rock a hundred times without so much as a crack showing in it. Yet at the 101st blow it splits in two. I know it was not the one blow that did it, but all that had gone before."* (not sure who penned these words)

I want to encourage you to not stop prophesying half way, just because you don't see anything happening. I want to remind you that God's words are like seeds, so once you send them out over your situation, you are planting them. You don't plant a seed today and reap a harvest tomorrow, or you don't plant a seed and then go the next day and dig it up to see the progress it makes. That is not how planting and reaping works...you have to plant the seeds; then there is a period of time that you have to wait, and then there is a harvest. Jesus in talking about the Kingdom and explains the parable of the seeds this way: *Then He said, "The kingdom of God is like a man who throws seed on the ground, and he goes to bed at night and gets up every day, and [in the meantime] the seed sprouts and grows; how [it does this], he does not know.* (Mark 4:26-27 (AMP). There is a time frame between the planting and the harvest; and in the same way prophesying has

99

to be an ongoing process, we send the words out and then we stay aligned in our confession to that seed, until it manifests. A farmer puts the seeds in the ground; he makes sure that the seed gets water, sunlight, fertilizers and he keeps the surroundings clean of weeds and thorns to ensure that his seeds have space and the right atmosphere to produce. But he never goes and disrupts the seed to see the progress. He trusts that once he does his part to protect the seed, God of the harvest will do the rest in bringing it to fruition. It works the very same way with the prophesying principle. The Apostle Paul gives us the same key, he said, *"Do not be anxious or worried about anything, but in everything [every circumstance and situation] by prayer and petition with thanksgiving, continue to make your [specific] requests known to God"* (Philippians 4:6 AMP). He is commanding us to stay in alignment with our prayer and prophecies, by continuing to be thankful and expectant, just like the farmer that puts his seed in the ground. When we remain consistent in our confessions and prophesying, what we are doing, in actuality, is protecting the seed that was first sown. You see, there is a thief, and his purpose is to steal and his eye is really on the seed that you are sowing because he knows very well that if he steals your seed, he can steal your life.

The problem in today's world is that we have not understood the power of the Word of God. We often think the enemy is out to steal our health, our money, our relationships, etc.; but the truth is, everything we need is wrapped up in the seed which is God's Word. I am passionate about getting this teaching out on the power of our words because I know it is the key to changing lives.

Jesus, in another parable, talks about the sower and the seed, and He explains that the seed is God's Word and the people are the different types of soil. (see Mark 4:13–12). As the seeds fall on these different types of soils, Jesus shows the disciples how the enemy comes and steals away the Word from them. The first set of seeds fall on the roadway and doesn't even have time to sink in and the devil snatches it away. The second set of seeds fall on rocky soil, and the seeds never get to take any root; they die because they could not handle the pressures and hardships of life. The third set of seeds fall among thorns, and the thorns are likened unto distractions and worries of the world that entrap us to keep up with fame, security, wealth and glamor. These worries sneak in and choke out the life of the seed. But, when he came to the last type of soil, he describes it as good soil and look at what he says, *"And those [in the last group] are the ones on whom seed was sown on the good soil; and they hear the word [of God, the good news regarding the way of salvation] and accept it and bear fruit—thirty, sixty, and a hundred times as much [as was sown]"* (Mark 4:13-20 AMP). I am giving you this Scripture to reiterate the point that once you protect the seeds of God's Word in your life, you will then be able to prophesy His words over your situations and circumstances; then there will most definitely be a harvest on the horizon. You must understand, beyond doubt, that continuous prophesy- ing is the key to protecting the seeds of God's Word in your life.

I know we would love circumstances to change in an instant, and sometimes our situations can be fixed with one touch from God, but most times it's a process, because we often need to learn how to build trust and confidence in Him. Not because you have gotten hold of the principle of prophesying will mean that everything will change overnight; in fact, it probably took years for the issue in your life to get to the stage it is in right now and, in the same way, it will take some time to reverse the process. It may seem long, and a bit difficult, at first, but don't give up prophesying because God's Word will come to pass.

Let us go on and look a little further into Ezekiel's vision now that we have a better understanding of the seeds we are sowing.

"So I prophesied as I was commanded; and as I prophesied, there was a [thundering] noise and behold, a shaking and trembling and a rattling, and the bones came together, bone to its bone. And I looked and behold, there were sinews upon [the bones] and flesh came upon them and skin covered them over, but there was no breath or spirit in them." (Ezekiel 37:7-8 AMP)

Ezekiel was obedient to prophesy, and as he did it, the words that came out of his mouth seemed to activate the bones in the valley. Ezekiel started to hear a noise and a shaking and in the vision he saw bone coming together and attaching itself to a bone. In other words, the bones started to be ordered by finding their place. In the same way, once you start prophesying God's Word to your situation, the first thing that will happen in your life is order; and the things that were looking cluttered will now start to conform and take shape as God intended them to be in the first place.

More and more science is proving God's Word to be true; and we see it especially in physics. In her book,

Quantum Faith, Annette Capps gives a brief comparison of quantum physics to quantum faith, she states, *"Words are energy and energy affects matter. The energy of your microwave vibrates the water molecules and heats the water. The energy of electricity flows to your washing machine and powers the motor that spins the tub and cleans your clothes. So, we can rightfully say that energy affects the matter in your life."* She also went on to say, *"When Jesus spoke to the fig tree and said, "No man eat fruit from thee hereafter forever" then that fig tree dried up from the atomic level because of His words. When He spoke to the winds and waves, they obeyed Him. He was teaching us the undeniable Biblical principle that THINGS OBEY WORDS."*

Now imagine with me all words are energy and energy affect matter. Matter is things we see and use every day like our cars, our computers, our desks etc. and they contain atoms. It is the atoms in the matter that respond to the energy of words, which brings change. I tell you this is revolutionary and amazing all at the same time. Now, let us go a step further and think about God's words being more powerful than any other words because they come from the mouth of God. Just imagine what those words in reality can do to effect change in your life. It is imperative that you reprogram your speech and don't stop speaking God's words. Now that we understand that words are energy and energy affects matter this would then give a clearer understanding as to why Ezekiel was able to prophesy and then there was a shaking; it was because the "bones" began to react to the energy of God's words being spoken. Don't you find it interesting that God told Ezekiel to prophesy, and God did not do the prophesying? God loves to partner with us so that

He can work through us in this earth realm, and today God still tells us to speak to our problems. Look at what Jesus said, *"For assuredly, I say to you, if you have faith as a mustard seed, you will say to this mountain, 'Move from here to there,' and it will move; and nothing will be impossible for you"* (Matthew 17:20b NKJV). I cannot emphasize enough that prophesying God's Word to our problems will cause the impossible to become possible. We just cannot deny the truth; words are very powerful!

As Ezekiel started to prophesy, he started to see traction in his vision, and as he kept looking at the bones intently, not only did the bones start joining, he saw sinews and flesh start to grow over the bones and then skin started to cover it. What an amazing miracle and this all started to happen because of the divinely inspired words he spoke, but I want you to look at what Ezekiel said after he saw some progress, *"But there was no breath or spirit in them"* (Ezekiel 37:8b AMP). The Scripture is a description of what happens when you start applying the prophesying principle in your life. Situations and circumstances will begin to change, and at first, it may not look like much is happening; in fact, it may look like nothing is happening at all, but just because you don't see anything, doesn't mean it's not happening. I am asking you to keep persistent in your prophetic declarations. You cannot prophesy God's Word one day, and then speak what you see in the natural the next day—you must remain consistent by standing on God's Word. In the fast-paced world we are living in, and the rate and speed of information circulating because of technology...patience, and consistency seems to be fast disappearing from our lives and everyone wants everything faster, but it is not

God's way; His way, most of the time, involves s‍
waiting. The Apostle James said, "My brethren, cou‍
all joy when you fall into various trials, knowing that the
testing of your faith produces patience. But let patience have its perfect work, that you may be perfect
and complete, lacking nothing" (James 1:2 – 4 NKJV). I
know it's not enjoyable to wait when the relationship is
bad, or the bills are piling up, or even when there is
pain in your body. But I also know God is faithful and if
He promised something it will come to pass as long as
you can believe and trust Him. Remember that in all
your trials God is still doing a good work in your life.

Double-mindedness Will Sabotage Your Progress.

Sometimes we tend to sabotage our progress by being
double minded, but if you are going to see changes in
your situations and circumstances you have to purpose
in your heart that you will not waver. The Apostle James
said, "If any of you lacks wisdom, let him ask of God,
who gives to all liberally and without reproach, and it
will be given to him. But let him ask in faith, with no
doubting, for he who doubts is like a wave of the sea
driven and tossed by the wind. For let not that man
suppose that he will receive anything from the Lord; he
is a double-minded man, unstable in all his ways
(James 1:5- 8 NKJV).

You can see the Apostle James addressing the way
we are supposed to make our requests to God. He
shows us we have to ask God for wisdom believing God
will grant us what we need. Once we are not doubting

but staying in faith that what we are asking for is based on his promises; we will get it. We all have been here, I know I was number one in being double minded and sometimes doubt still tries to creep in, but I'm learning how to trust God more. There was a time; I admit that I prayed according to God's promises to see my church filled with people on Sunday mornings. In the moments of prayer, I was full of faith, I felt the service would be packed out but as I would come out of prayer I would say to my husband things like, "I don't think we will have a good turnout today." Or "With this weather I don't think people will want to use public transport, so I doubt many people will come." Or "Don't prepare too many cups for communion because I don't anticipate a big turnout." Do you see how I was double minded? And let me tell you, just as I said it the results followed and then I would sit there is church confused as to why this was happening. Being double minded means that we don't stay in faith in our prophesying after we have made our request to God. We pray the answer but as soon as we leave his presence we speak all the negatives in the natural thereby nullifying our prayers and sabotaging ourselves and we blame the devil or God for not working things out for us. James says, "For he who doubts is like a wave of the sea driven and tossed by the wind. For let not that man suppose that he will receive anything from the Lord; he is a double-minded man, unstable in all his ways" (James 1:6b-8 NKJV).

Have you ever gone to the beach and just sat on the shores and noticed the waves? I am sure that if you have you would have noticed that the wave's movement has a lot to do with the direction of the wind. In whatever the direction the winds blow the waves move accordingly, and James likens a person who doubts like a wave having no sure direction but being dictated by the wind. When you move away from prophesying God's word, then you will be subjected to the situation and circumstances that life throws at you. For example, pain in your body will dictate the way you live your life whether you will be happy, joyous, sad or mad. A lack of money will drive you to frustrations and hopelessness. An unhappy marriage will drive you to adultery or alcohol. And James says, "For let not that man suppose that he will receive anything from the Lord; he is a double-minded man, unstable in all his ways" (James 1:7-8 NKJV). Let not which man? The double minded man; he will not receive his answer because he is unstable in his ways. I truly believe this is why many of our prayers go unanswered because of our inability to stand strong even when we do not see the natural signs lining up with the promises of God. We give up too soon and walk away because it seems to be taking too long.

Let us go back to Ezekiel "And I looked and behold, there were sinews upon [the bones] and flesh came upon them and skin covered them over, but there was no breath or spirit in them" (Ezekiel 37:7-8 AMP). The great prophet Ezekiel had to go through the process of being consistent. Imagine if Ezekiel just stopped and walked from the scene leaving the job half way done, it would have proven to be a huge disappointment to God and his fellow men that were going to benefit from his consistency. I'm very thankful that he stuck it out because he was half way through to seeing God's word come to fruition. I want to encourage you more than ever not to give up; I want to go further than encourage you I want to plead with you, please do not give up because you just might be half way through to your miracle.

The Spirit Gives Life to Your Prophesying

Then said He to me, "Prophesy to the breath and spirit, son of man, and say to the breath and spirit," Thus says the Lord God: "Come from the four winds, O breath and spirit, and breathe upon these slain that they may live." So I prophesied as He commanded me, and the breath and spirit came into [the bones], and they lived and stood up upon their feet, an exceedingly great host (Ezekiel 37:9-10 AMP).

It is amazing to see first Ezekiel prophesied to the dried bones and as he did, great progress took place and the bones were taken care of but still there was more to be done, and God told him to keep prophesying but this time not to the bones but the breath and spirit. You see as long as we keep speaking God's words and promises over our dead situations like our health, our finances, our relationships, our loved ones and so on God will always allow life to come by His Spirit. Truly it is only God that can make the impossible - possible and what is so beautiful about all of this is we get to be a part of it. Today we have been given the Holy Spirit, and He is there to help us especially when we do not know how to pray or prophesy. Holy Spirit was there from the beginning and is here today doing the same work, making known the power of Jesus, who is the actual word of God. Dr. David Yonggi Chow in his book "4th Dimensional Living in a 3 Dimensional World" states, "Words spoken with the help of the Holy Spirit are always creative, productive, and powerful, and they likewise, will become manifest in the third-dimensional realm." Why don't you take time today to ask Holy Spirit to come into the darkness of your situation? Ask him for help; ask him for guidance and clarity, I know he will help you. I can only imagine the emotions Ezekiel felt when he prophesied and before his very eyes the huge pile of bones took on form and flesh and then came alive and stood up! I probably would have passed out slain in the spirit from a scene like that, and that is the problem; the unbelief and the doubts that God can bring back the dead things to life. As you are reading this book at this moment, I want you to take a few moments and just ask God for help to believe him and to take him at his word. If we are going to see great miracles and experience great power in our lives, we will first have to believe radically like the men of old. The men of old did not have the Holy Spirit living in them like we have today, so we are even more privileged than they were. The Apostle Paul describes Abraham this way,

"We call Abraham "father" not because he got God's attention by living like a saint, but because God made something out of Abraham when he was a nobody. Isn't that what we've always read in Scripture, God saying to Abraham, "I set you up as father of many peoples"? Abraham was first named "father" and then became a father because he dared to trust God to do what only God could do: raise the dead to life, with a word make something out of nothing. When everything was hopeless, Abraham believed, deciding to live not by what he saw he couldn't do but on what God said he would do. And so he was made the father of a multitude of peoples. God himself said to him, "You're going to have a big family, Abraham" (Romans 4:17 – 18 MSG)!

I pray that we would be people that will dare to believe God for the dead and broken pieces of our lives to come together again as Abraham did.

Prayer of Creative Words

Father, give me the strength and tenacity to keep on the track of prophesying today, help me not to grow weary or discouraged in this process.

Father, today I will not allow the enemy to steal my seed, I will stay focused on your kingdom, and your words and I say fear, lack, fame, worry of getting more or keeping up with the world will not have any place in my life.

Father, today I decree and declare that my heart is plowed and ready for the seed of your word to bring change to my life and to produce a progressive harvest, first thirty, sixty and finally one hundred fold.

Father, today I have gained knowledge that words are energy and energy affect matter; with this understanding I will now begin to release your words that are more powerful than any others words in the world, and I know my dry bones will come to life.

Father, I am setting my heart and mind on your word, I refuse to be like the wave of the sea being driven and tossed by the wind but rather today I declare that my mind is sound, stable and fixed in your words of life.

Father, today I have decided I will no longer sabotage myself and my future by being double minded. I declare that my confession all through the day will line up with my prayers and petitions.

Father, I ask as I remain consistent in my prophesying the Holy Spirit will come and hover over my dead situations even as He did when the earth was void of formless. May the Holy Spirit infuse life into the words I speak and cause every bit of darkness, chaos and confusion to be removed from me!

Father, today I will stay steady, strong and immovable on the words of God because I know I cannot live without your words. I speak all these declarations in Jesus name; Amen!

WORDS

Chapter 9

Believe it, Say it, Have it

You Will Have What You Say

And Jesus, replying, said to them, "Have faith in God [constantly]. Truly I tell you, whoever says to this mountain, Be lifted up and thrown into the sea! and does not doubt at all in his heart but believes that what he says will take place, it will be done for him" (Mark 11:22-23 AMP).

These are some very powerful words spoken by Jesus and therein holds the principle and pattern for this journey call life. One day Jesus and His Disciples were on their way to Jerusalem, and while on their way Jesus was hungry. From a distance, He saw a fig tree and thought He could get something to eat from the tree; but as they got closer to the tree, it was all green and full of leaves, but no fruit was on the tree. The Bible tells us that, at that moment, Jesus spoke to the tree, *"And He said to it, No one ever again shall eat fruit from you. And His disciples were listening [to what He said]"* (Mark 11:14 AMP). After these words were spoken, they continued their journey to conduct their business. The next morning, they were passing by the tree again, and

Peter noticed that the tree was dried up at the roots. He reminded the Lord that the day before He had cursed the tree and that's when Jesus turned to them and spoke these powerful words, *"And Jesus, replying, said to them, Have faith in God [constantly]. Truly I tell you, whoever says to this mountain, Be lifted up and thrown into the sea! and does not doubt at all in his heart but believes that what he says will take place, it will be done for him"* (Mark 11:22-23 AMP).

The first, and foremost, aspect of the creative process is to have your speaking grounded in God—your belief, trust, and confidence must be in him. Now, if you are not grounded in Him, your words will still produce, but the results will not be the "God kind" of results; never-the-less it will produce. The first thing Jesus commands the Disciples to do is *"Have faith in God [constantly]"* (Mark 11:22b AMP). When you speak God's words, you are having faith in the One who said it and trusting the One who said He'd perform it. The responsibility to bring it to pass is all up to God, but your responsibility is to believe He can perform His Word, and trust me He can! But how do we continue to have faith in God when things are falling apart at the seams?

The Apostle Paul tells us in the book of Romans, *"So faith comes by hearing [what is told], and what is heard comes by the preaching [of the message that came from the lips] of Christ (the Messiah Himself")* (Romans 10:17 AMP). Again, this Scripture proves to you that your belief system is all based on the words you hear. So the more of God's Word and Promises you intake, the more faith you will have in Him to perform according to your speaking. If you keep listening to lies from the enemy, then you will speak in line with fear, making the enemy your "source"; and I have to reiterate nothing good will ever come from him. If you keep listening to other people's opinions about your life, then you will live and speak accordingly, thereby making other people your "source." It is imperative, at this juncture, that you stop and take stock! Ask yourself, "Whose words have I been listening to?"—the answer to that question will lead you to the source of all that is happening in your life. Once you correct the main source to your belief system, then you can begin to correct the speaking pattern, and let me remind you again it will take time for the process of negative speaking to change to positive...so please be patient along the way. God will always back up the person who will dare to believe Him and trust in His words.

There is a wonderful story in the Old Testament that I love, and the principle of speaking is evident all over it. It's the story of Elijah and the widow of Zarephath. Let us look that this in some detail.

And then this happened: Elijah the Tishbite, from among the settlers of Gilead, confronted Ahab: *"As surely as GOD lives, the God of Israel before whom I stand in obedient service, the next years are going to see a total drought—not a drop of dew or rain unless I say otherwise"* (1 Kings 17:1 MSG).

Elijah was a prophet of the Old Testament, and in my opinion, one of the most powerful. He moved with great power and authority, and from the Scripture, you can see clearly the confidence with which he operated. Look at the first part of his statement, *"As surely as GOD lives, the God of Israel before whom I stand in obedient service,"*—Elijah was able to speak with such confidence because he established His source as God, just like Jesus told His Disciples *"Have faith in God [constantly]"* (Mark 11:22b AMP). Elijah understood his source and with that understanding the confidence that his words would be fruitful flowed. Elijah spoke the words commanded by God and those words became his words. He immediately became the mouthpiece for God's will to be done on earth. God's Word, in his mouth, would now control the material earth realm because Elijah then says in the last part of the verse, *"The next years are going to see a total drought—not a drop of dew or rain unless I say otherwise"* (1 Kings 17:1b MSG). His understanding of who he was connected to enabled the material world to obey his words. Jesus also describes this principle,

"I am the Vine, you are the branches. When you're joined with me and I with you, the relation intimate and organic, the harvest is sure to be abundant. Separated, you can't produce a thing. Anyone who separates from me is deadwood, gathered up and thrown on the bonfire. But if you make yourselves at home with me and my words are at home in you, you can be sure that whatever you ask will be listened to and acted upon. This is how my Father shows who he is—when you produce grapes, when you mature as my disciples" (John 15:5-8 MSG).

Jesus was stating the same principle to His Disciples that Elijah followed. We have to stay connected to the source because the truth is we draw life and sap from what we are connected to, and then in turn produce from that very source. So, at this point, I am hoping you realize that the majority, or all that is happening in your life, has a lot to do with what or who we are connected. It is my prayer that we would be able to come to the place where we can be like Elijah, being able to command the natural realm with our words and see it obey.

After he announces this drought for three years, God leads him away to hiding east of the Jordan by the brook, Cherith, where he would have water to drink and God personally fed him by the Ravens (See 1 Kings 17: 2-6). It takes real faith and trust in God to live like this; but, again, it has to do with the knowledge of the source. After a while, the brook started to dry up and then God brought further instructions to Elijah. God did not give Elijah all the instructions at once, but the instructions came bit by bit, as Elijah remained obedient to every step. In the same way as you begin to reconstruct your speech, by staying connected to God's Word you will begin to trust God step by step, and you will notice you are not so preoccupied with the future by worrying about it but you will find yourself waiting for the next set of instructions expectantly. Life will begin to get more enjoyable rather than endurable. Let us look at what God told Elijah next,

And the word of the Lord came to him: Arise, go to Zarephath, which belongs to Sidon, and dwell there. Behold, I have commanded a widow there to provide for you. So he arose and went to Zarephath. When he came to the gate of the city, behold, a widow was there gathering sticks. He called to her, Bring me a little water in a vessel, that I may drink. As she was going to get it, he called to her and said, Bring me a morsel of bread in your hand (1 Kings 17: 8 - 11 AMP).

Elijah was obedient to God's instructions, and as God said it to him, it was exactly so. I want to remind you God's Word will never fail, and it will always come to pass if we remain in faith. But what follows next is astounding; the widow's perspective and words,

And she said, "As the Lord your God lives, I have not a loaf baked but only a handful of meal in the jar and a little oil in the bottle. See, I am gathering two sticks, that I may go in and bake it for me and my son, that we may eat it—and die" (1 Kings 17:12 AMP).

There is a very powerful principle tied up in this verse, and many of God's children are missing it and are operating by the opposite of the principle, even today. The principle hidden in this verse is "thankfulness for the little" will always lead to multiplication that in turn will yield life. So instead of the woman thanking God for the little she had, she despised it and in doing so, she released death words. When our perspective is small we will speak small or diminishing words, and that shuts up the heavens for God to move in our situation. Jesus used this same principle of thankfulness for the little,

Then He ordered the crowds to recline upon the grass, and He took the five loaves and the two fish, and, looking up to heaven, He gave thanks and blessed and broke the loaves and handed the pieces to the disciples, and the disciples gave them to the people. And they all ate and were satisfied. And they picked up twelve [small hand] baskets full of the broken pieces left over. And those who ate were about 5,000 men, not including women and children. (Matthew 14:15-21 AMP).

Jesus' prayer of thankfulness for the little fed about 20,000 people that day, if we were to take the women and children into consideration. This principle will cause the heavens to open, and miracles will happen with your little paycheck or the little food in your cupboard, the little money in your pocket book, the little time you have with your family, and that little business you own. I'm hoping you get the gist of the principle. When we understand this principle, many things will begin to change in our lives, and our words will become life, instead of death. Keep this in mind, "Thankfulness opens the door for multiplication that leads to life, complaining diminishes the little and leads to death!"

As long as there is life, there is hope. The widow had a small perspective, and she spoke death words, but never-the-less, she followed the instructions given to her by Elijah,

Elijah said to her, Fear not; go and do as you have said. But make me a little cake of [it] first and bring it to me, and afterward prepare some for yourself and your son. For thus says the Lord, the God of Israel: The jar of meal shall not waste away or the bottle of oil fail until the day that the Lord sends rain on the earth. She did as Elijah said. And she and he and her household ate for many days. The jar of meal was not spent nor did the bottle of oil fail, according to the word that the Lord spoke through Elijah (1 Kings 17:13-16 AMP).

The simple act of obedience, on behalf of the widow, saved their lives and fed them for a long time. Elijah helped to change the perspective of the woman by showing her when we give to God first, even out of the smallest amount, we open the door to miracles. Now, after this miraculous event in the widow's life, things started to take a turn for the worse and it seemed to come out of nowhere. I mean, here we see the mighty hand of God move so powerfully in the midst of famine, where there was no way to buy food or replace the flour and oil in the jars. Yet every day when she went to prepare meals there was always flour and oil available. God kept providing and multiplying, according to the prophet's words, and the simple act of obedience of the widow; yet, disaster was about hit. Why would God multiply and provide and feed and then do this?

After these things, the son of the woman who was a mistress became sick; and his sickness was so severe that there was no breath left in him. And she said to Elijah, *"What have you against me, O man of God? Have you come to me to call my sin to remembrance and to slay my son"* (1 Kings 17:17-18 AMP)?

Here we see what seems to be a waste of a miracle because the widow's son dies, and when this happens, she goes to Elijah the prophet and accuses him of this tragedy. Isn't this ironic and so much like us? So many times in our lives God brings us out of a mess, God sends help, God works miracles, God makes a way where there was no way...and then something goes wrong, and we fly in God's face and accuse Him of being cruel to us, or we accuse Him of punishing us for our sins. Does this sound familiar? I've done this so many times in my life it is too numerous to count. But, I want to bring something back to your attention, it's what the widow said in verse 12 earlier,

"And she said, As the Lord your God lives, I have not a loaf baked but only a handful of meal in the jar and a little oil in the bottle. See, I am gathering two sticks, that I may go in and bake it for me and my son, that we may eat it—and die" (1 Kings 17:12 AMP).

120

Look at her words, *"That I may go in and bake it*
and my son, that we may eat it—and die" (1
17:12 AMP).

The widow released the words of death into the
atmosphere, not only over her life but in the life of her
son. I believe as she saw the goodness of God from His
provision, daily, her faith might have grown, and she
probably started to think and speak differently, but the
words that she so recklessly released over her son was
still in effect. Her words activated death, and yet she
blamed the prophet. Like this widow, many of us have
failed to realize that our words are so potent and so
powerful and the words hold creative substance that
once we release them they will eventually manifest. The
good news is that this woman, once she realized the
greatness of the prophet, even though she blamed
him, decided to bring her son to him for healing. Without hesitation, he did all he could to revive him. Depending upon God, Elijah was able to bring the boy
back to life (1 Kings 17:19 - 24 AMP). There is hope when
we return to God, and when we learn to apply the
truths of God Word to our lives. Yes, we are regular
people, but what makes us powerful are the words we
speak by divine inspiration. The Apostle James describes the same powerful prophet Elijah this way,

Elijah was a human being with a nature such as we
have [with feelings, affections, and a constitution like
ours]; and he prayed earnestly for it not to rain, and no
rain fell on the earth for three years and six months. And
[then] he prayed again and the heavens supplied rain
and the land produced its crops [as usual] (James 5:17-
18 AMP).

Elijah, with the divinely inspired Word of God, controlled the material realm, and James describes him as being just like you and I. Isn't that powerful and hopeful? It's not too late to start speaking God's Word over your life, situations and circumstances that seem like mountains in your way. God's Word is powerful when spoken by faith. I also want to go a step further to prove to you, you will have what you say. I just shared with you a Bible story of how powerful our words are, but I also want to share with you my experience with words.

Watch Your Words

In my introduction to this book, I told you that there was a series of events with negative effects that was happening in my life, and I did not understand why. I know I am a woman of prayer and a child of God, but the events still took place in my life, and it led me to ask God, "Why?" Remember His answer was only three words to me, "Lisa your words!", and those words have led me to this finished product. Well, I never really got around to telling you what those events were, and that was intentional. I wanted to lay the groundwork for the power of *your* words so *you* would have a full understanding of what takes place when you speak words, recklessly.

In the year 2008, the economy was hit with a very bad recession and people on every level were affected. People lost their jobs, their homes went into foreclosure, and many businesses had to close their doors that resulted in layoffs of employees. It was a very dark time for us all in America. As a result of this dark period, I found myself listening to the lies of the enemy that seemed to be magnified every minute of the day throughout all the media. It seemed to me as if we lived in a world that only focused on all that was wrong and negative, the unemployment rate was rising, the debts that our country was acquiring was huge, the reports focused on social security not being available for the next generation and homelessness was rampant. But what was strange about this whole scenario is the more I listened to the negative reports, the more I was drawn in, and without realizing it, I found myself gripped by crippling fear.

I kept tuning into all the negative reports to get more information about the current state of affairs, because we also owned a small business that was affected. The lies of the enemy were magnified in my mind, and from day to day, month to month, it seemed to grow darker and worse in my mind. Even though I tried to speak positive words and kept a positive outward appearance, there was no peace on the inside. Internally, there was a storm of worry raging; major crippling fear would grip my heart. I started playing death scenarios and failure images over and over in my mind. All the while, having no idea the damage I was doing to myself, based on reports I was listening to. I chose to believe the news, rather than the Word of God. Mind you, all the while, God in His grace was taking care of us, providing for us, and the recovery process was happening for the nation, as well as for us. It may have seemed slow, but it was sure, but because of roots of lies being in my heart from words I constantly heard, I could not see the goodness of God through it all.

Once lies take root in your heart, if they are not pulled out, it will eventually produce bad fruit. Even while I was trying to speak God's Word, I still had the root of worry, fear and anxiety internally and my mental picture of my life and health was very far from positive. In essence, what happened was my little time spent in the Word, and prayer was not effective because I was now rooted stronger in the negatives of what I heard and believed. Sure enough, the roots of worry started to manifest itself in my body, and the first thing I noticed was my hair started falling out, and this only triggered further death pictures and because I was so consumed with my natural circumstances—the roots went down deeper and deeper. And this is exactly how the enemy works—he capitalizes on opportunities in the believer's life when they are most vulnerable by planting a negative thought or image in their mind. Once we receive that thought and never use the Word of God to replace it, then the opportunity for roots to grow is ripe. And this is what happened to me, after a few years my belief pattern became so distorted and negative that I started saying over and over to myself, "I feel I will get a stroke one day!" and "I feel like I will just drop down and die!" I also found myself being consumed with accident thoughts while driving, and I started voicing those thoughts out loud to myself. I remember, at times, just playing the whole scene out in my mind of how I will die in a car accident and then I would say, "One day I will just get in an accident and die." I know, it sounds crazy just writing it now, but, the reality is that I started sending those words out into the atmosphere for a few years constantly. Of course nothing happened right away, so I just kept right on saying it, and it became sort of a joke. I remember in the summer of 2013, my friend had a birthday party for her daughter, and I was preparing to go. As I was preparing, I started to get terrible pains on the right side of my neck, shoulder and arm, and jokingly I said to my friend, "Even if I am getting a stroke I will be there for that party so don't worry, I am coming!" Thinking back now with all the wisdom and knowledge I have gained from the principle of words, it is really by God's grace I am here writing this book. Two days later the pain was still there, so I decided to drop my kids off at my friend's house and visit the doctor. As soon as the doctor's assistant checked me out and tested my blood pressure I saw a state of panic on her face even though she was trying to remain calm...I felt something wasn't right. She told me to try and relax and then she tested it again and again and again. Then she called the doctor, and he tested my pressure it was 204 over 116. I was in the danger zone of a stroke. Yes! A stroke...you heard me! Immediately, the doctor sent me to the emergency room at the hospital and then a follow-up visit that eventually led me to be diagnosed with hypertension and now dependent on medication to control it. One would think with this close call to death I would have wised up, but during the time this was happening it had not dawned on me that I was speaking these things into existence, and now more so, I kept saying how bad I was feeling. In fact, I couldn't wait for someone to ask me how I was doing so I could go on and on elaborating about the fact that I almost got a stroke. And instead of fixing the problem, I talked more and more about it, which resulted in my having a stronger belief that I was going to die. I started to believe I was going to die and the devil wanted to kill me, I became very depressed, and I couldn't stop myself from thinking about death.

Hypertension was just one more fact to add to continue the downward spiral of death thoughts. I eventually got the boldness one day to call my Pastor and speak with him, and I remember telling him how depressed I was feeling and the thoughts and dreams that consisted of my death. I remember him praying for me and encouraging me to think and speak life, but to no avail. I kept down the path of "death" words. I started to realize that I was stressed all the time, and I was very impatient with my family and the words that spewed out of my mouth were very poisonous and detrimental to my future and my family. But, I just kept right on perpetuating a belief system of death by my constant words of death. Finally, a day came when the very words I prophesied manifested itself in a terrible car wreck with my two children and me. By God's grace, we all came out unscratched but that was the pivotal moment in my life when I went before God and asked him why were all these things happening to me? That's when he said to me, "Lisa your words!" His words not only changed my life but saved my life, I believe now that if God did not speak those words to me I would not be here. I was fast digging my own grave with the death words I was speaking. I am very thankful that God answered me that day, and though His words were few, it led me to this place of clarity and knowledge as to why my life seemed to be falling apart. I want you to understand that your words are not only going to affect you but those close to you as well so please give more thought to the words you speak. Since coming into this knowledge of words I have made every effort to correct my path and I try to watch my words carefully because I know I can bring life or death with them. I have told you it will take some time to get this process going, so don't get discouraged when you don't see the answers immediately. I can assure you though, that if God did it for me, He will most definitely do it for you; don't give up because I know if you follow the patterns laid out in this book you will begin to see dead bones come to life and doors of never-ending miracles open for you. I trust that you have been blessed by this read, and as I go, I want to leave you with the following Scriptures for meditation. Please continue to SPEAK LIFE!

Meditation Scriptures

Death and life are in the power of the tongue, and they who indulge in it shall eat the fruit of it [for death or life]. Proverbs 18:21(AMP)

For let him who wants to enjoy life and see good days [good—whether apparent or not] keep his tongue free from evil and his lips from guile (treachery, deceit).
1 Peter 3:10 (AMP)

A soft answer turns away wrath, but grievous words stir up anger. Proverbs 15:1 (AMP)

Let no foul or polluting language, nor evil word nor unwholesome or worthless talk [ever] come out of your mouth, but only such [speech] as is good and beneficial to the spiritual progress of others, as is fitting to the need and the occasion, that it may be a blessing and give grace (God's favor) to those who hear it.
Ephesians 4:29 (AMP)

But I tell you, on the day of judgment men will have to give account for every idle (inoperative, nonworking) word they speak. For by your words you will be justified and acquitted, and by your words you will be condemned and sentenced. Matthew 12:36-37 (AMP)

There are those who speak rashly, like the piercing of a sword, but the tongue of the wise brings healing.
Proverbs 12:18 (AMP)
Let the words of my mouth and the meditation of my heart be acceptable in Your sight, O Lord, my [firm, impenetrable] Rock and my Redeemer.
Psalm 19:14 (AMP)

A gentle tongue [with its healing power] is a tree of life, but willful contrariness in it breaks down the spirit.
Proverbs 15:4 (AMP)

If you have read this book and realized that you don't know Jesus as you Lord and Savior and you would like to make him your Lord it is very simple...just pray the simple prayer below in faith and this will mark the beginning of a new life in Christ.

Prayer for Salvation

Heavenly Father, I come to You in the name of Jesus. I have recognized, and I acknowledge that I am a sinner, and I am in desperate need of a Savior. I repent for my sins and the life that I have lived that has not been pleasing to You. I need Your forgiveness, Lord. I believe Jesus is the only begotten son of God and that He died for my sins. I confess Jesus as the Lord of my soul, I believe in my heart, and I confess with my mouth that Jesus died and rose from the grave, and I now make Him my personal Savior. I want to thank You, Lord, for saving me and giving me eternal life. Amen!

Bibliography

Websites:

Bert, Peggy. (September 30, 2010). Peggy Bert. In Simple Steps to Elevate Life and Relationships. Retrieved undefined, from http://www.peggybert.com/2010/09/30/positive-and-negative-words/.

http://www.ask.com/world-view/many-words-speak-day-68b7ff8bd0b6943e

http://www.foodsafety.gov/poisoning/effects/index.html#

Ebooks:

Brizendine, Louann. *The Female Brain*. New York: Morgan Road, 2006. ebook.

Capps, Annette. Quantum Faith. England, AR: Capps, 2006. ebook.

Cho, Yong-gi. *4th Dimensional Living in a 3 Dimensional World*. Orlando, FL: Bridge-Logos, 2006. ebook.

Hagin, Kenneth E. *Words*. Tulsa, OK: K. Hagin Ministries, 1979. ebook.

Trimm, Cindy. *Commanding Your Morning*. Lake Mary, FL: Charisma House, 2007. ebook.

Trimm, Cindy. 'Til Heaven Invades Earth. N.p.: n.p., n.d. ebook.

Webster's New Collegiate Dictionary. Springfield, MA: G. & C. Merriam, 1973. ebook.

Vine, W. E., and W. E. Vine. Vine's Concise Dictionary of Bible Words. Nashville: T. Nelson, 1999. ebook.

About the Author

Lisa Singh is the pastor of
Heavenly Grace Ministries in New York
and the bestselling author of
Created on Purpose for Purpose.
She is the host of Living the POP Life—
*People of Prayer believing
in the Power of Prayer*...
aired weekdays on
www.globespanradio.com
Lisa lives in Queens with her husband
and two children.

www. hgmny.org

99565667R00074

Made in the USA
Columbia, SC
09 July 2018